BRACES
A consumers guide to orthodontics

BRACES
A consumers guide to orthodontics

By G. Ray Callahan, DDS MS
Diplomate of the American Board of Orthodontics

Cover consultant - Pam Sather, BFA

1stBooks – rev. 6/26/01

TABLE OF CONTENTS

List of Illustrations vii

Why Children and Adults May Need Braces ix

General Considerations for Parents and Adult Patients 1

Chapter One
> Symptoms You Can See.. 1
> What to Expect When You Call for an Appointment 14
> The Ten Most Important Questions for the Orthodontist . 14
> After the Records, How Do You Decide?.......................... 23
> Why Braces Are Expensive. 24
> Orthodontic Insurance.. 25

Chapter Two
> Orthodontic Tooth Movement 27
> Treatment Sequence.. 28
> The Pain Factor with Braces 29
> Safety in the Dental Office 30

Braces for Children Ages Five through Seventeen............. 35

Chapter Three
> The Concept of Early Treatment....................................... 35
> Growth and Treatment Timing 36
> The Importance of Patient Cooperation 37
> Thumbsucking and Other Habits 41
> School, Athletics and Appointments................................. 45

Chapter Four
> Cleft Palate Treatment 47
> Extraction or Non-extraction?.. 49

Braces and Faces.. 51
Functional Appliances 52

Braces for Adults Over Age Eighteen.................................. 55

Chapter Five
Adult Orthodontics.. 55
Current Facts and Fads about Braces............................... 56
Orthognathic Surgery.. 59
TMJ – What Is It? 60
The Invisalign System... 62
Lingual Braces 63
Treatment Motivation Survey 66

Forms You Might Need To Sign.. 71

Chapter Six
Medical /Dental History.. 72
Federal Truth in Lending Disclosure Statement for
Professional Services 74
Informed Consent for the Orthodontic Patient................. 75
Orthodontics.. 75

The Orthodontist 85

Chapter Seven
How to find an Orthodontist 85
Ethical Considerations 87
The Orthodontic Team 87

Conclusion 91

Glossary of Orthodontic Words and Terms 93

Acknowledgments... 97

LIST OF ILLUSTRATIONS

Illustration		Page
Figure 1	Normal Tooth Anatomy	xi
Figure 2	What you might see in the mouth	2
Figure 3	Lower arch	3
Figure 4	Anterior Crossbite	4
Figure 5	Very Large Spaces	5
Figure 6	Severe Overbite and Overjet	6
Figure 7	Severe Crowding	7
Figure 8	Missing Tooth	8
Figure 9	Missing Lateral Incisors	9
Figure 10	Crowded teeth and anterior open bite.	10
Figure 11	Same Case After Correction	11
Figure 12	Mixed Dentition Case Before Treatment	12
Figure 13	Same Case After Treatment	12
Figure 14	Generalized Spacing Case	13
Figure 15	Same Case After Treatment	13
Figure 16	Fixed (or glued in) Lower Retainer	20
Figure 17	Low Pull Headgear	38
Figure 18	Directional Force Headgear	39
Figure 19	High Pull Headgear	40
Figure 20	Thumbsuckers	42
Figure 21	The Pacifier	43
Figure 22	Twin Block Functional Appliance	53
Figure 23	Edgewise Brackets Without Archwire	56
Figure 24	Edgewise Brackets With Archwires	57
Figure 25	Lingual Braces	64
Figure 26	Lingual Braces, Front View.	65

Why Children and Adults May Need Braces

We all know that personal appearance is very important. It is especially so during the formative years when a child's or adolescent's self-esteem is most vulnerable to the negative attention of peers. Adults who did not have their crooked teeth corrected earlier are also very concerned with their appearance. Business careers frequently are affected by such situations. Even your speech may be affected by teeth either out of line or severely rotated. It is a commonly known fact that cavities go hand in hand with crooked teeth. Very crooked teeth cannot be properly cleaned by brushing or by your dentist or hygienist. If an individual's teeth are so crooked that others notice them, it is cause for concern. The search for a solution to this problem often leads to the orthodontist to have the teeth straightened. Even though you want the teeth to be straightened to improve your appearance, the orthodontist knows that improved function will be an additional benefit. The teeth are placed in the arch so that they preserve each other by deflecting food into proper areas which do not promote cavities or gum disease. With straight teeth comes an increase in the efficiency of the chewing function. Correct alignment aids tongue and lip placement for proper speech. It will even help your teeth last a lifetime. While appearance is very important, longevity is important also. After all, the teeth must withstand the pressures of chewing. Your teeth determine how well you can chew and what you eat determines the nutrition you receive. Having and preserving a healthy chewing system is critical to good health. In today's society many people are facing important questions regarding their dental health and appearance. Does my child need braces? Do I need braces? Can I afford them? What do they do? Are they painful? How long do patients wear them? Can a person be treated at any age? These are just a few questions that confront the family when your dentist says, "I want you to see an orthodontist".

Normal Tooth Anatomy and Alignment[1]

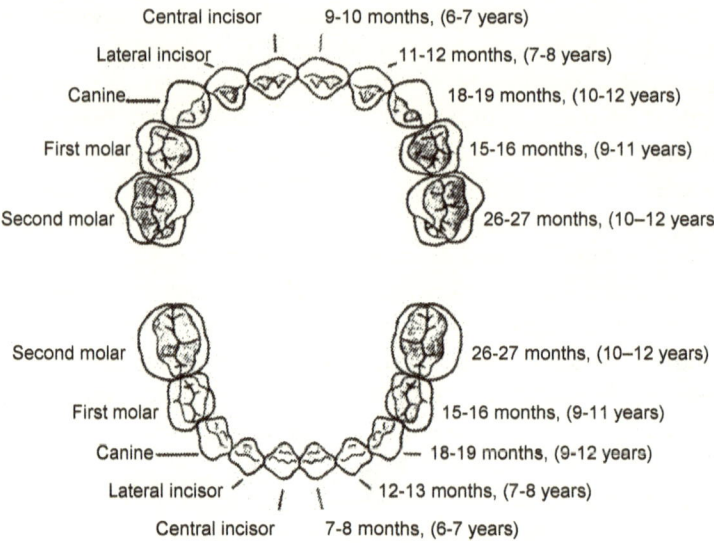

Central incisor   9-10 months, (6-7 years)

Lateral incisor   11-12 months, (7-8 years)

Canine   18-19 months, (10-12 years)

First molar   15-16 months, (9-11 years)

Second molar   26-27 months, (10–12 years)

Second molar   26-27 months, (10–12 years)

First molar   15-16 months, (9-11 years)

Canine   18-19 months, (9-12 years)

Lateral incisor   12-13 months, (7-8 years)

Central incisor   7-8 months, (6-7 years)

The Primary Teeth

The average age when the teeth erupt are shown.
The ages in parentheses are the average ages when they fall out.

[1]Rebecca W. Smith, *The Columbia University Guide to Family Dental Care* (New York, London: W. W. Norton & Company) p.15.

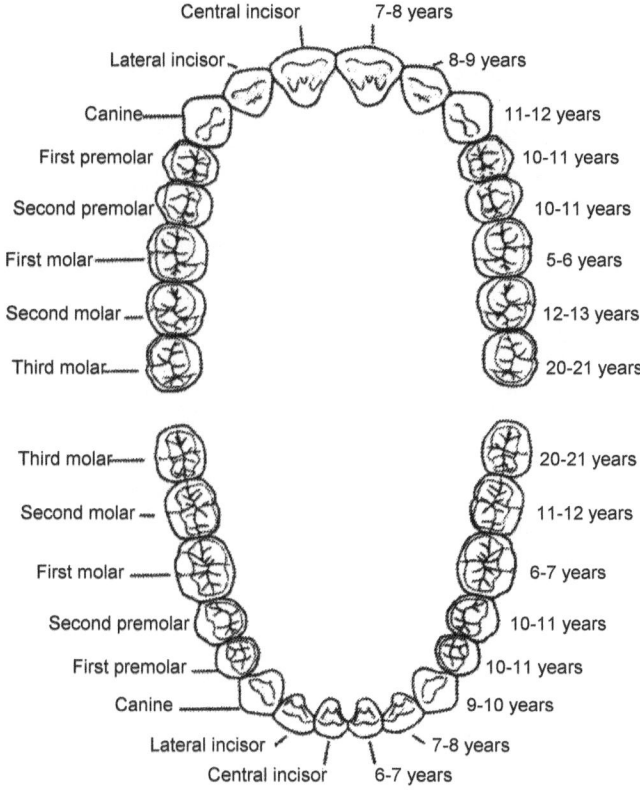

Central incisor — 7-8 years
Lateral incisor — 8-9 years
Canine — 11-12 years
First premolar — 10-11 years
Second premolar — 10-11 years
First molar — 5-6 years
Second molar — 12-13 years
Third molar — 20-21 years

Third molar — 20-21 years
Second molar — 11-12 years
First molar — 6-7 years
Second premolar — 10-11 years
First premolar — 10-11 years
Canine — 9-10 years
Lateral incisor — 7-8 years
Central incisor — 6-7 years

The Permanent Teeth

The average ages when they erupt are shown.

Figure 1 Normal Tooth Anatomy

General Considerations for Parents and Adult Patients

Chapter One

Symptoms You Can See

Before I explain some symptoms that you can see, let me tell you what it means to have normal teeth and occlusion (how your teeth bite together). Normal teeth are not just blobs of enamel. Each tooth in a symmetrical arch has a particular shape and function. Where each tooth touches its neighbor is very precisely positioned to create support and allow food to move around it in definite fashion. The precise movement of food allows it to slide off the teeth without sticking (and eventually causing cavities) and the food massages the gums between the teeth to promote healthy gingiva (gums). Teeth and their supporting structures are naturally arranged to fulfill their function of properly chewing food and also to improve their longevity. The orthodontist tries very hard to rearrange all the teeth in the manner that nature intended. In addition to the alignment of teeth in the arches, the teeth must be positioned so they hit their opposing teeth correctly. This also makes their chewing actions more efficient. Another variable is the size of the opposing arches. No matter how straight and well positioned the teeth are in the arches, if the arches do not relate to each other properly, occlusion can never be normal and the teeth can't protect themselves.

Before making an appointment with an orthodontist, you may want to have a close look at the teeth about which you are concerned: your own, your child's or both. Even though you're not a dentist there is no reason why you shouldn't take a look. Many children frown on their parents looking into their mouths, but you can see many things very easily to help make a decision.

1

Most of the time your child will be very anxious to have braces. That should help you get a look.

To start, let's try the old teaspoon trick. You don't have to be a dentist to do this. Adults can do it for themselves by standing in front of a bright mirror. For a child, have him or her sit on a chair facing you and directly in front of you. Hold regular (clean) teaspoons by the bowl with your fingers. Act like you are leading the orchestra. Have the child say "Ahhhh", and slowly put the spoon handle inside each cheek. Gently move the spoon handle sideways to pull the cheeks away from the teeth. With the mouth still open, look at the alignment of the teeth. They should be in a smooth U-shape from one side to the other.

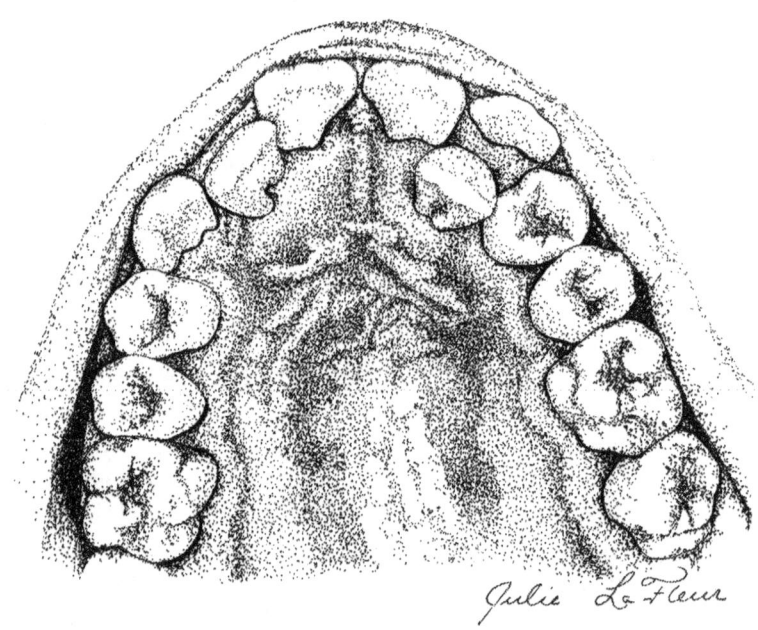

Figure 2 This is what you might see in the mouth. Note the teeth out of line.

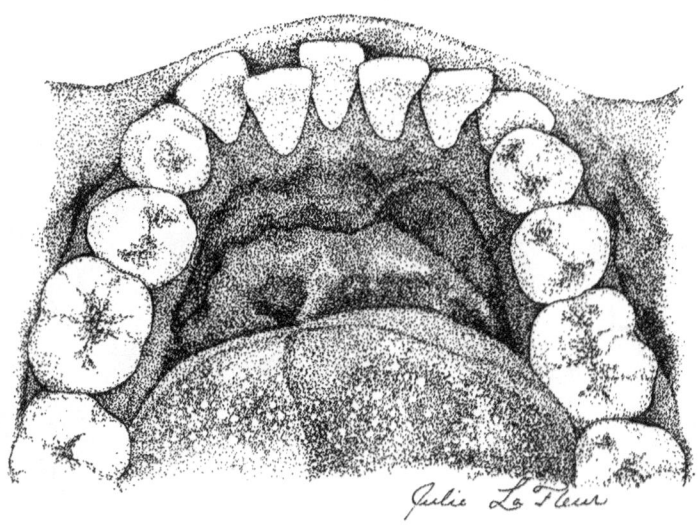

Figure 3 Lower arch. Note the large first molar at the back of the arch. If your child is over six years old this tooth is not a baby tooth. It must last a lifetime. Don't delay if it has a cavity.

You can also see if some teeth are turned one way or the other. If you see any teeth erupting in the roof of the mouth or even a lump in the tissue, you need to see an orthodontist. The lump might be a permanent tooth trying to erupt.

Have your child bite the teeth together and hold them that way. Are the upper teeth biting outside the lower teeth? They should be. If the lower teeth on one side or both sides or all around are biting outside the upper teeth, then your child has a crossbite. Crossbites interfere with normal chewing functions so they are considered functional problems, and should be corrected as soon as practical. After you have seen your child's teeth, ask if they would like to see yours. Let them hold the spoons and repeat the procedure.

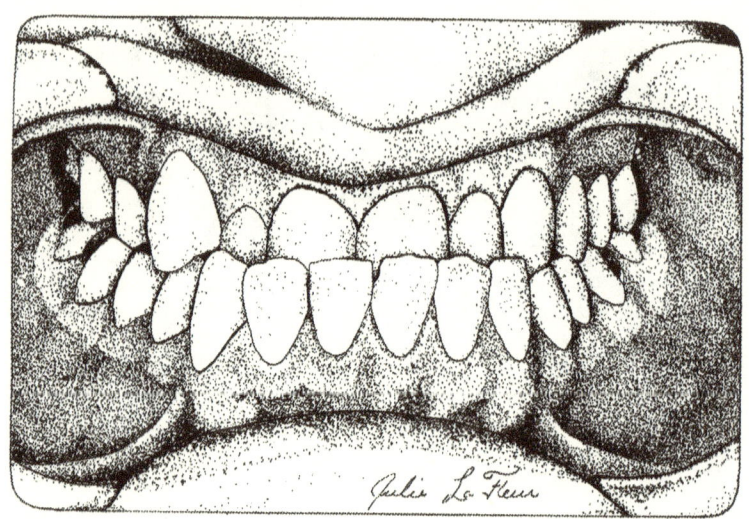

Figure 4 Anterior crossbite. Lower teeth outside the upper teeth.

When the lower teeth are in front of the upper teeth, it is not normal, but it can be corrected. Are there teeth protruding through the gum above the upper teeth? Are essentially all the teeth crooked?

Ask your child to open his or her mouth again so you can look for spaces between teeth. Some space is good at certain ages, but bad at others. If the child has some permanent teeth and some baby teeth in his or her mouth then he or she should have some spaces between the front two or maybe four teeth. These spaces allow for the eruption of the permanent teeth that are larger than the baby teeth. When the child has mostly permanent teeth there should be no space between the upper

4

front teeth. If your child has spaces, the orthodontist will mention it, and you can acknowledge that you noticed it.

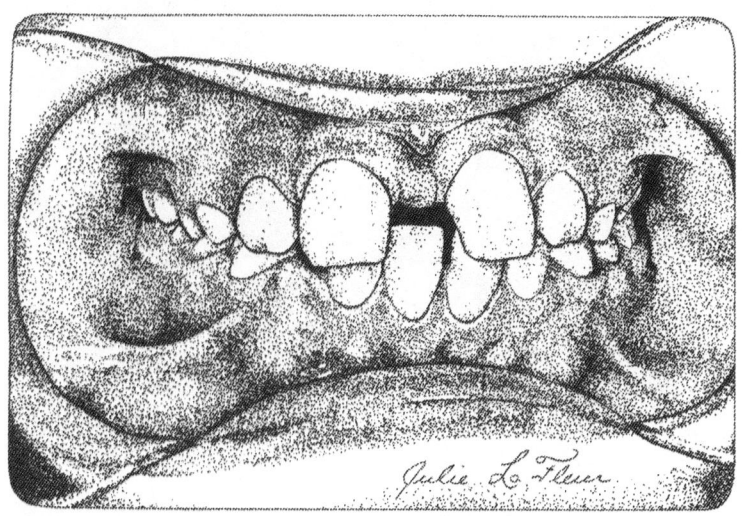

Figure 5 This shows a very large space between upper central incisors. This is not normal and the person should be seen by a dentist or an orthodontist.

If you see holes in teeth, then you need to see the general dentist right away. Orthodontics can't be done with cavities present or they will get worse during treatment. Strange little tissue bumps on the side of the gums are not normal either. They are probably small abscesses coming from an infected baby tooth. Abscesses require the services of your general dentist or pedodontist. It will be better for the child if this problem is dealt with sooner rather than later.

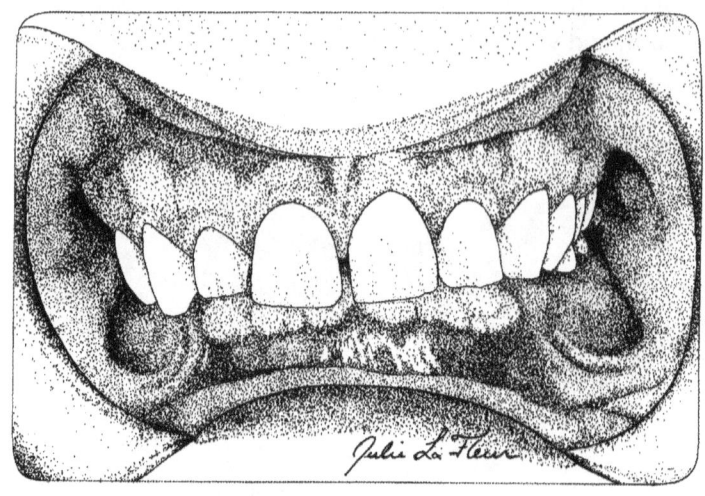

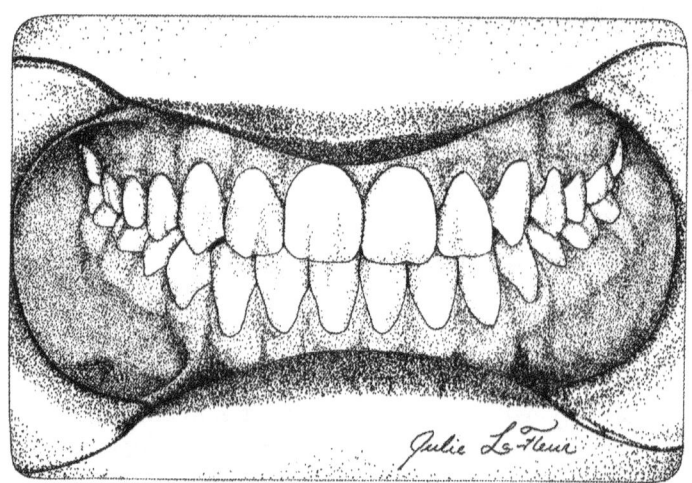

Figure 6 Severe overbite and overjet. No lower teeth are showing. Lower picture shows the same case after correction.

Do the gums bleed when you brush? Are they red and puffy? Are the teeth exceptionally dirty and does your breath smell bad? You might have periodontal disease. It is always a good idea to have a dental checkup with your regular dentist before you see the periodontist or the orthodontist. The specialists will not do the same things that your dentist does so there will be no duplication of services. Look for the white edges of teeth starting to poke up through the gum just inside the other teeth. This may be an extra tooth or a permanent one that erupts under a baby tooth that didn't come out because it was ankylosed (grown to the bone). When you or your child bite the teeth together, do the top teeth stick out a significant amount over the lower teeth? If so, that can be corrected.

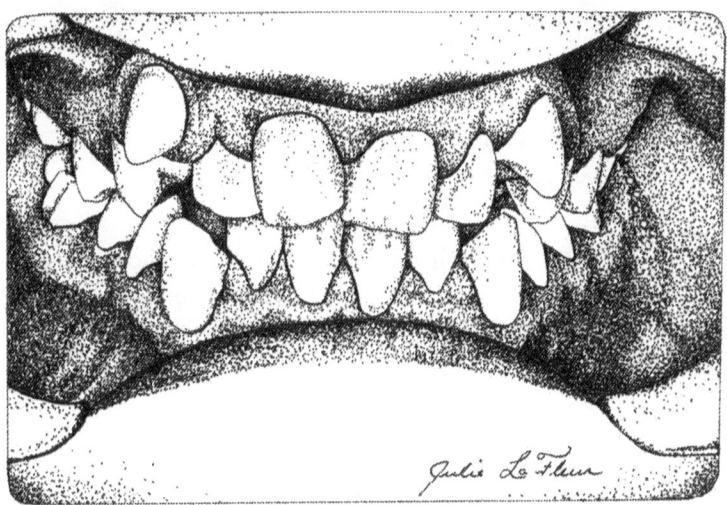

Figure 7 Severe crowding. Canine teeth erupting through the gum above the arch line.

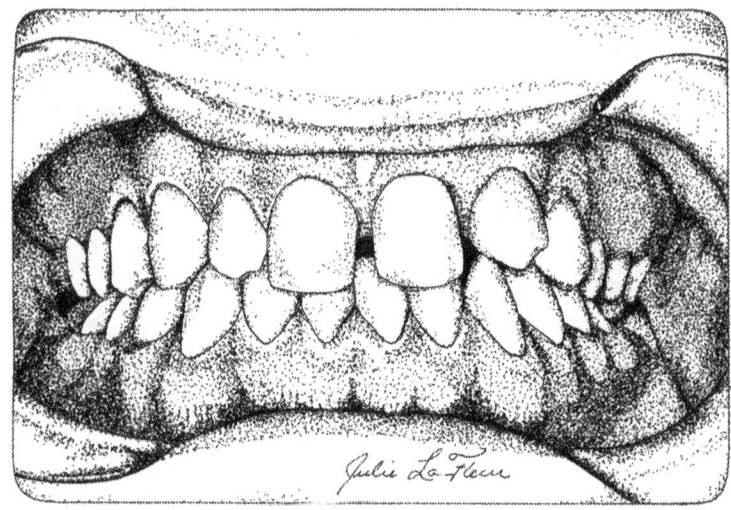

Figure 8 Missing tooth between upper left central incisor and the upper left canine.

Occasionally teeth will be missing in other places. The most common teeth to be missing at birth are the upper lateral incisors. This condition is very commonly inherited from parent to child.

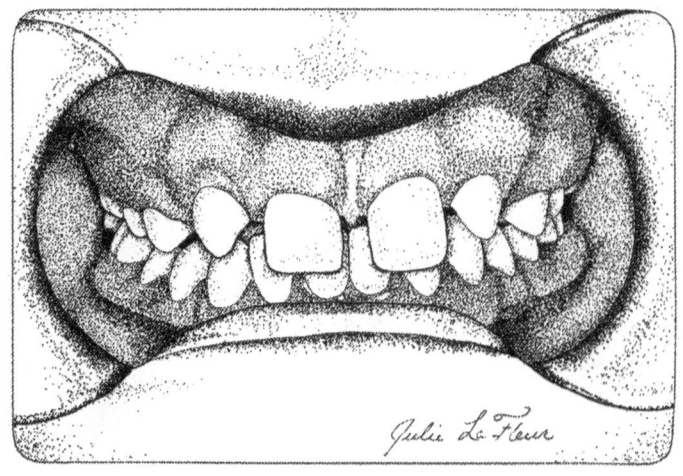

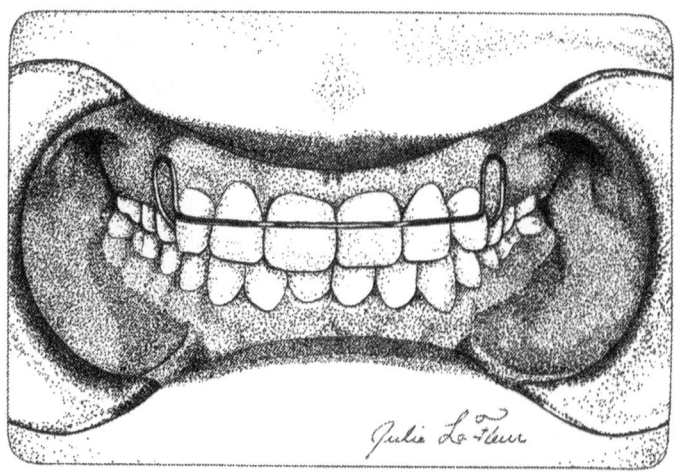

Figure 9 Upper drawing - both upper lateral incisors missing. Lower drawing - same case after braces. Missing teeth have been replaced on the retainer during the retention period. Permanent replacements will have to be made by your general dentist.

9

African-American patients have gingiva that looks a little different from Caucasians because of deposits of melanin in the tissue. It has no effect on treating the case. Treatment is basically similar for everyone. This African-American patient had four premolars removed and the chip on the front tooth was ground off to improve the appearance.

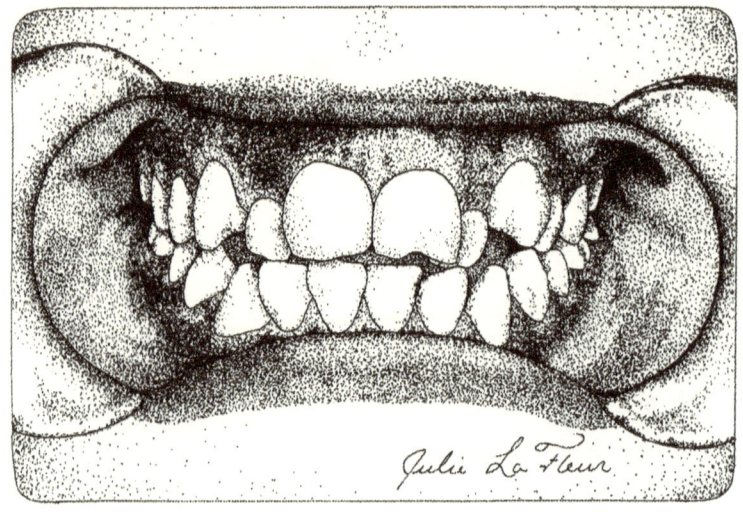

Figure 10 Crowded teeth and anterior open bite.

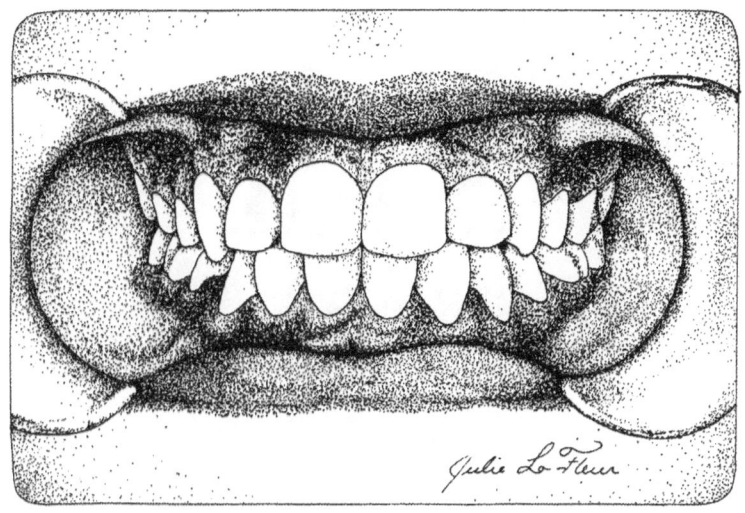

Figure 11 Same case after treatment - four teeth were extracted.

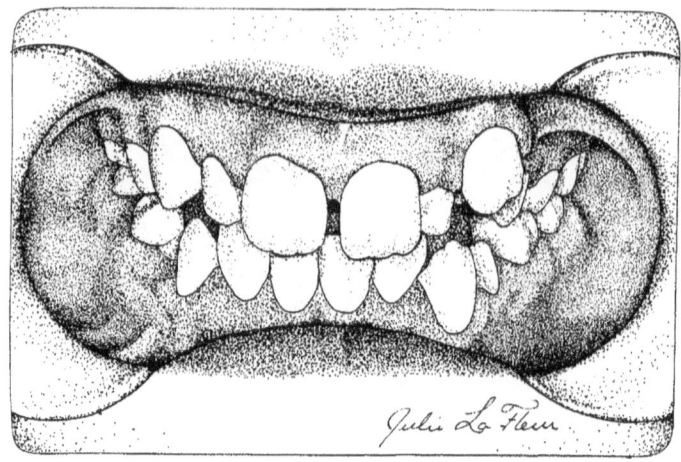

Figure 12 Mixed dentition case (some baby teeth, some permanent) with anterior space and crowding.

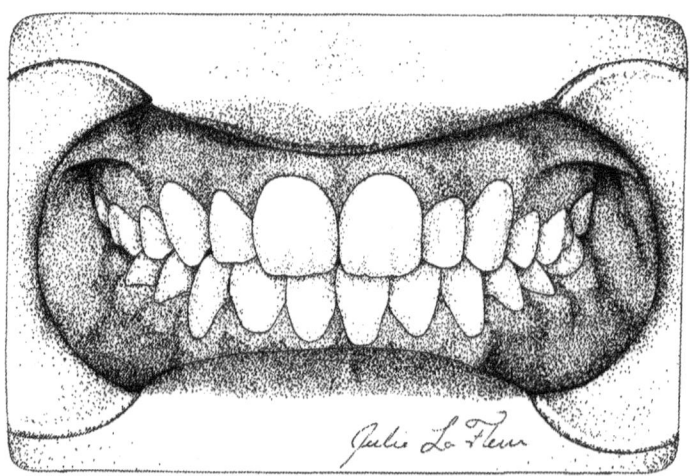

Figure 13 Same case as above after correction - four bicuspids extracted.

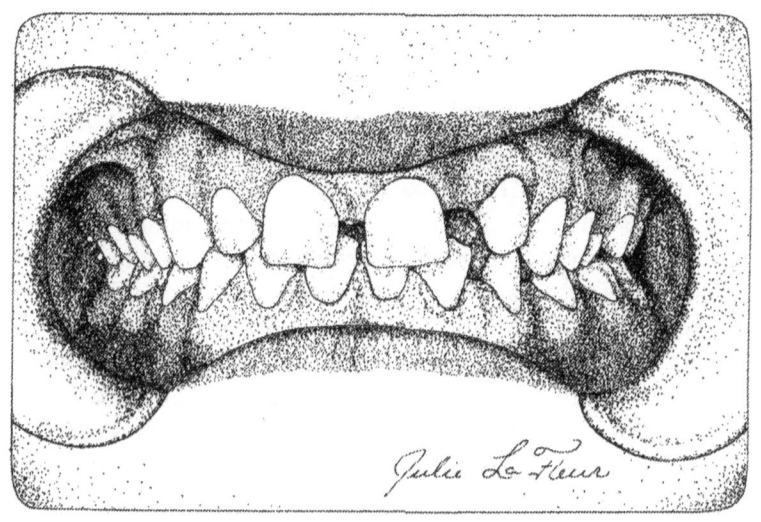

Figure 14 Generalized Spacing Case

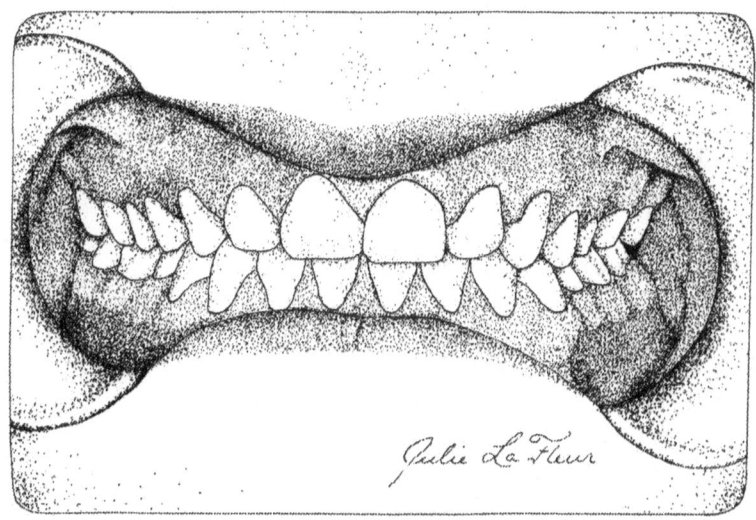

Figure 15 Same Case After Treatment - nonextraction.

What to Expect When You Call for an Appointment

A friendly receptionist will answer the phone, and after it is determined that you want to make an appointment for yourself or your child, you will be asked several questions. Among them will be the patient's name, address, phone number, and the responsible party's place of employment, social security number, insurance carrier, and referring dentist or other person if there is one. If you are a single parent they'll also want the same information for the child's other parent. As I stated before, you don't have to be referred to an orthodontist; anyone can call and make an appointment to be seen. Many orthodontists don't charge a fee for the initial examination, but they should tell you if there will be a fee. They will also tell you details about what you can expect at the first appointment, where the office is and how to get there efficiently. If they want you to get any x-rays from your general dentist they may ask you to bring them or they may call and get them for you. Anyway, they will answer all your questions and ease your mind about the appointment.

The Ten Most Important Questions for the Orthodontist

1. What Is Wrong With These Teeth?

Your general dentist has probably given you some idea of the problems, but the orthodontist should be more precise about what is wrong, and what is right about the teeth. He or she will tell you which teeth are crooked (although that may be obvious), whether the bite is normal or not, and whether teeth are erupting early, on time or are delayed. He or she will also be able to determine whether space is inadequate or excessive, whether a growth problem is apparent, or anything else that is pertinent. Any periodontal problems especially for adults will be discussed at this time. Problems with the bite relationshiip of the teeth or even lip, tongue or thumb habits may also be discussed at this time. These conditions occur in all people regardless of race or ethnic background. Treatment is equally effective for all.

2. What Can Be Done to Correct the Teeth?

"Braces" is not a sufficient answer. The orthodontist should be happy to tell you the general treatment plan. It can't be very specific until they have taken complete records (x-rays, study models, etc.), but they should be able to give you an idea about what they have in mind. Will extractions be needed (teeth pulled), or headgear and rubber bands need to be worn? How important will cooperation from the patient be to the final result? Even the type of braces should be discussed, because there are more of them all the time. If any periodontal treatment is needed, it will probably have to come first. Sometimes they can be done together. Of course any necessary fillings would have to be done before orthodontics.

3. How Long Will the Correction Take?

Most orthodontists say the correction process takes two years. That is for the average active treatment (braces). Most full cases (full upper and lower braces) take from eighteen to thirty months to complete. If the patient is in an active growing stage the treatment proceeds faster. In adults and non-growing children it takes a few months longer. How much does the patient's attitude affect the length of treatment? It is very important that the child knows his or her cooperation increases the speed and efficiency of the treatment. If the patient has a two-phase treatment it means a longer overall treatment time, but there will probably be a break of several years between the phases. After the active treatment there is an inactive (or retention) stage of treatment which takes about the same amount of time. After the first six months the retainers are usually worn just at night, so patients don't feel like they are wearing braces for that long. Actually, it is very important that patients wear some appliance (braces or retainers) for at least four years.

4. When Should We Start?

Every orthodontist loves the "when do we start" question because he or she assumes that you are ready to start. But not so fast, let's consider some questions that will help determine the child's or the adult's readiness. Have all periodontal questions been answered by the periodontist? Are all the permanent teeth showing in the mouth? Will they be erupted at least six months before the case should be finished at two years? Would there be any benefit in waiting for physical or emotional development? If the process requires phase one, is this the very best time to start? Would it help you, financially, if the treatment could be delayed for a year or two without compromising the case? If the patient is not quite ready some people start monthly payments right away and when the patient is ready, there is no initial payment due. It makes it a little easier to handle the fee.

It is not necessary for all permanent teeth to be erupted before treatment is started. Orthodontists want to be confident that all permanent teeth including second molars will be erupted before they complete the case. If some teeth don't erupt on time the treatment may be extended just to let those teeth erupt. Patients don't like that because they want to be finished, and neither do the orthodontists because they usually don't get paid extra for an extended treatment time. Everyone benefits if the starting time is delayed enough for the doctor to feel assured all permanent teeth will be in place by the time he or she needs them.

5. How Much Will the Correction Cost?

Do not ask the cost question first! All cases are not the same and all fees are not the same. If you insist on knowing up front, you could get a higher fee estimate. Most orthodontists are somewhat flexible as fees go. They will usually give you a fee range and then suggest that their assistants go ahead and get full orthodontic records on the patient so that a complete diagnosis can be done. Orthodontists are reluctant to work with you on a lower fee unless they know exactly what they're going to do. You can understand that. If you are fairly comfortable with the orthodontist and the fee, you could go ahead and let them do the records. If you want to schedule it for another time, that is your option. Whenever you do it, there will be a fee for the records. They do not come under the free initial exam.

Orthodontists usually work on a flat fee basis. That means they will give you a definite fee amount to complete the case. With this system there is incentive for the doctor to complete the case within the projected time. Of course a certain percentage of cases cannot be finished on time for whatever reason, but the orthodontist usually doesn't get extra pay if that happens. Some cases finish early but the fee is not usually decreased unless it is more than three months early because that offsets some of the many cases that run a few months over. If the case finished six months early, I always adjusted the fee. Of all the variables, missed appointments are the biggest source of delayed finishing dates.

6. Do You Have A Finance Plan with Payments?

When the cost comes up, you may be handed over to the financial secretary. That's probably a good idea. Be sure to ask what is expected for the down payment, how much the payments will be, and how long they will last. A good question to ask is whether there is a finance charge. I'm afraid that most orthodontists do charge interest these days because they have found that the accounts coming into the household that charge interest get paid before those not charging interest. An orthodontic practice is still a business with employees and overhead, and if you want the treatment, the charges must be paid. Occasionally you may not be able to meet your arranged payment. What happens then? In my office, my bookkeeper rearranged the payment schedule as necessary to keep the patient coming for the appointments. If the parent can't keep up the regular payment, they may stop bringing the child in for adjustments. When that happens the treatment may be prolonged, and that is undesirable for everyone. Even on a longer payment schedule, the doctor would prefer to keep the patient on the regular treatment regimen so he or she can be finished on time. The patient will benefit greatly.

There are many payment plans in every office. If you are able and want to save some money, you can pay the fee in advance. The orthodontist may give you a 5 to 10% discount for cash. If you're not comfortable with that, don't do it. Prepayment is just one of many payment options. Two responsible parties may be paying the fee in a given case if the parents are divorced. Be sure to ask if it will be a problem if that is your situation. It really is no problem if your doctor uses a computer. I have had patients come to me because I had a computer, and their previous orthodontist couldn't or wouldn't do it. I once had a mother bring in three children with different last names, and their fathers each paid their child's fee.

7. What Happens If The Orthodontist Gets Sick?

You need to know what arrangements have been made with other doctors to take care of your child should your orthodontist become sick or disabled. Fortunately, the American Association of Orthodontists furnishes forms for legal and ethical agreements which allow them to cover each other's practices. Your orthodontist should be able to tell you who he has agreements with, and how they would proceed. It is possible to allow all patients to skip an interval without serious problems. In practice, the treatment continues even though the wires are not adjusted every time. When I was having major surgery one time, I just moved all my appointments ahead six weeks. At the end of that time, I resumed my practice and everyone was happy. I had written an explanatory letter to every patient telling them why I would be gone for that period.

8. Is the Treatment Area Open?

I am a firm believer in having an office where the patients are treated in an open area. The patients seem more at ease when they can see the orthodontist treating other patients. Orthodontists don't do anything that other patients or parents should not see. I wanted my patients to see me working on other patients without hurting them. Most parents are a little apprehensive having any doctor interact closely with their child over so long a period of time. I liked working on children out in the open where parents could see the procedures. Patients liked to see and talk to each other, and that tended to make them more comfortable. My chairs were in a circle, and children could converse with each other while waiting their turn. It sounds like there is a lot of waiting, but that is part of it. After I glue a bracket or whatever in the mouth, it needs several minutes to set. That allows me to work on another patient. With experience it goes very smoothly and no one waits too much.

9. What Are Retainers and How Long Do I Wear Them?

Many types of retainers are in use today. The original retainer was designed by a doctor named Hawley so they are called Hawley Retainers. They consist of plastic areas in the roof of the mouth and inside the lower teeth with wires across the front of the upper and lower teeth. These wires allow some pressure to be put on those teeth if some spaces need to be closed after the braces come off.

19

Hawley retainers are regularly used in cases where teeth have been extracted because the wires with their adjustable loops furnish a way to adjust the pressure to keep the extraction spaces closed.

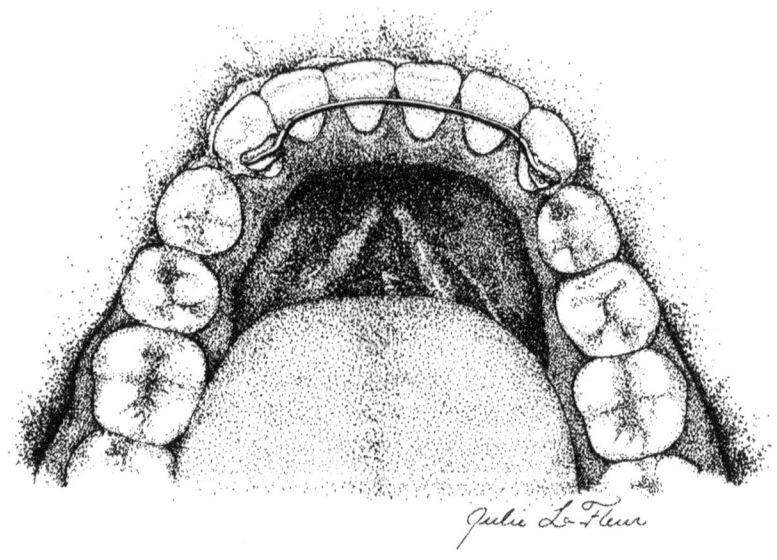

Figure 16 Fixed (or glued in) lower retainer.

In cases where no teeth were extracted the upper Hawley is still used, but the lower is different. It is usually a "fixed" retainer that is glued to the lower front teeth on the inside. Non-extraction cases usually need support on the outside of the upper teeth and on the inside of the lower teeth. Two-tooth retainers can be glued on the inside of any two teeth that the orthodontist feels might want to move apart. These are most commonly found on the inside of the two upper front teeth because they frequently have spaces before treatment starts.

A clear plastic retainer that fits precisely over all upper or all lower teeth may also be made. It is usually referred to as an "invisible" retainer. It is not invisible, but it is hard to see at a glance. It holds the teeth in place very well, but is not easy to keep clean. When it's dirty, it looks bad and is likely to cause cavities and bad breath.

Another retainer some doctors use is called a "tooth positioner". It is made of rubber or flexible plastic and is constructed on a plaster model of the patient's teeth which have been cut off the model and realigned in wax. The flexibility of the positioner allows it to stretch over the newly aligned teeth and gradually move them to the predetermined position. This process sounds very good and it is, but it only works if the patient wears it according to the doctor's instructions. That means it must be worn for four hours during the daytime and slept in throughout the night. Wearing it only at night will not do the job. The four hours of daytime wear with the constant biting down on it every twenty or thirty seconds is critical to success. The hazards with this retainer (actually it is an occlusion finishing device) are many. All the braces must be removed in order to construct the positioner so if the patient doesn't wear it exactly as prescribed, the teeth move very quickly toward previous crooked positions. This results in the need to put the braces back on and refinish the case before regular retainers are made. That may add up to six more months of treatment which makes no one very happy. Needless to say orthodontists are reluctant to place a tooth positioner except for their most responsible patients.

In some cases retainers are necessary until the wisdom teeth (third molars) erupt during the late teen years. You should know what the charges are for retention, lost retainers and broken retainers. Does the retention period last until the wisdom teeth have erupted or have been removed? By the way, if wisdom teeth have to be removed, that surgery is performed by an oral surgeon, not by your orthodontist.

There may be a separate fee for the retention period. Sometimes that is the only way to make people appreciate the importance of the retainers. The end result will be compromised if retainers are not worn as prescribed by the doctor. Any child or parent who ignores the retainers will be disappointed by the final result. Sometimes children are less than accurate in their explanations to parents. In my office we always made sure a parent either was there for delivery of retainers or was sent a sheet of instructions through the mail. We also found a retainer a few times in the bushes outside of our office where a patient had "lost" them even before going home.

10. What Orthodontic Records Are Needed For Diagnosis?

Orthodontics has come a long way from when a dentist took a quick look at your child's teeth and said, "We will do this and that". Virtually every orthodontist is now university trained, and aware of the tremendous advances that modern science has given us.

Recent advances in radiography as well as computer aided imaging has enabled the orthodontist to make more accurate diagnoses and projection images that show the patient just what treatment can do. All of these wonderful developments have not replaced the basic set of records that are obtained in every case.

All orthodontists want the following records:
- a. A thorough medical history including "Treatment Motivation Survey"
- b. Plaster study models of your child's teeth (newer methods allow a scanner to make a three dimensional projection of all the teeth. I think it will be awhile before most offices have that kind of a computer. It may happen in the future.)
- c. X-rays - panoramic - shows all of the teeth
  cephalometric - shows head in profile
  hand film - helps judge skeletal age (optional)
- d. Facial Photographs - frontal and profile view
- e. Intraoral photos - show pictures of the teeth
- f. Periodontal charting of gingival attachment

These procedures are usually done by orthodontic assistants who are trained for this purpose. The impression for study models is done with a tray, like a funny shaped spoon or scoop with some soft material that looks like cake icing in it. The assistant puts it in the patient's mouth for about fifteen seconds and then it comes out with a little suction, and it's done. The new scanner is like putting a mouth mirror in the mouth and around the teeth. The x-rays and photos are very easy and not frightening. Dentists measure the depth of gingival pockets around the teeth and then construct a chart of these bone levels. This is done painlessly with a dental instrument that all dentists use.

After the Records, How Do You Decide?

The next appointment will be a consultation where the orthodontist will sit down with you and go over each record. He or she can tell you how a diagnosis was determined. It should be very clear what the orthodontist proposes to do and exactly what it will cost. You can ask questions. If you are uncomfortable with the fee or any of the answers to these questions, you don't need to do anything at this visit. Tell the doctor you want to postpone a decision until you have discussed it among yourselves. After you get home, include your child in the decision making process. If you decide you want to continue, call the office and make the appointment to start.

Don't wait too long to call because your records might go into storage at another site. If you decide not to start with this orthodontist, just call and tell the receptionist. Your next step should be an appointment with the second orthodontist on your list. There is nothing wrong with seeing another orthodontist. Even after you have had records taken, you can have the office send those records to another orthodontist to get his opinion about how he or she would treat your child. The orthodontist who takes the records must be paid for them, and probably before you can take them to another orthodontist. By the same token, the next orthodontist should deduct the cost of the records from his fee if he treats your child. After you pay for the records, they belong to you, but the orthodontist may not want to give them directly to you for fear of loss or damage. He does, however, have to send them to any other doctor you wish. I assure you, this will not be a problem.

Why Braces Are Expensive.

I'm sure that many of you would like to know why braces are so expensive. Of course, it is a combination of factors. An orthodontic education is increasingly expensive, requiring three or four years of undergraduate college, four years of dental school, and two or three years of graduate school in orthodontics. Nine or ten years of college add up to an incredible expense. Mine took many years to pay off even that long ago. After an orthodontist becomes licensed, he or she must rent and equip an office. You can roughly figure about $70,000 to set up an office with only one patient chair. Our x-ray machines cost at least $20,000. Additional kinds of supplies and small equipment items are needed plus a continual supply of brackets and wires. Needless to say, it adds up to a sizeable sum. When you add that to the rent (which could be $20 to $40 per square foot per year or more) and the staff salaries, I'm surprised that anyone has the nerve to start on their own. Actually, most young orthodontists do go in with an older practitioner to start. Then they eventually buy the office. It must be obvious that the orthodontist's staff will want to set up definite arrangements as to how you are going to pay the fee. Like it or not, the orthodontist has to run the practice like a real business, because it is. The banks expect the doctor to pay the bills on time. All these costs create a monetary overhead that the orthodontist has to produce every month to stay in business.

Orthodontic Insurance

Insurance coverage for braces is becoming more popular all the time. Dental insurance is certainly not as common as medical insurance, and only a portion of dental coverage includes orthodontics. In most cases an insurance company will assign a certain amount of money for braces rather than a percentage of the total fee. In some situations a company will allow a certain percentage up to a maximum of so many dollars. For instance, when the company assigns a dollar amount of coverage they will usually allow amounts ranging from $750 to $2,000. The balance of the fee will then be the responsibility of the parent or guardian. On a percentage basis the company might allow 50% of all charges up to a maximum of $1,000 or $2,000. Insurance doesn't pay the whole fee, but it helps the average family afford to have the treatment.

The American Association of Orthodontists helps families finance braces with a program called "Direct Reimbursement". In this situation the employer pays a certain amount of money directly to the adult or parents to reimburse them for payments to the orthodontist. There is a maximum amount here also, but the company and the adult or parents get more for their money, because the middle-man (insurance company) is eliminated. Needless to say the insurance companies do not approve of that plan.

Not every insurance company has dental or orthodontic coverage; but if enough people ask for it, it will become routine. My advice would be to ask your employer to look into Direct Reimbursement. Further information can be obtained by writing the American Association of Orthodontists at 401 North Lindbergh Blvd., St. Louis, MO. 63141-7816.

G. Ray Callahan, DDS MS

Chapter Two

Orthodontic Tooth Movement

The movement of teeth in an orthodontic case is fairly simple. Putting pressure on the tooth with brackets and wire causes this pressure to be transmitted to the root of the tooth. The root is held to the bone by a fibrous membrane called the periodontal ligament. The pressure on the tooth root causes the ligament to be compressed on one side of the root and stretched on the other side. On the side of compression, certain cells called osteoclasts are stimulated to form, and they proceed to start eating away the bone on that side. On the stretched ligament side, cells called osteoblasts are formed and they start adding bone. The eating away of the bone on the pressure side proceeds faster than the adding on of bone on the stretched ligament side, so the net result is that the membrane space around the tooth root enlarges. This is why teeth undergoing orthodontic movement tend to be loose. It is also why retainers are so important because the teeth need to be held in place until the bone grows back in where it should be to hold the tooth in place.

If the teeth are not kept very clean some bacteria and debris may be able to get into the membrane space and cause an infection that causes some of the bone and ligament to be lost. A pocket is created which attracts more bacteria and a permanent defect is located next to the tooth. These problems must be corrected by the periodontists who specialize in treating gum disease. They can perform many miracles, and work hard to keep people from losing teeth. If any active periodontal disease is present in a pending orthodontic case, it must be treated and corrected before orthodontic treatment. Moving teeth with braces tends to make gum disease worse, so we all have a vested interest in making sure that it is corrected before the orthodontist starts the case.

Treatment Sequence

If the average orthodontic case takes two years to complete, the timing of the treatment goes something like this. The examination, orthodontic records, and the consultation appointment take about two months to complete. Putting on the brackets, wires, and headgear, if necessary, takes about five appointments over three months. The next six months are usually taken up with arch wire changes. The last eight or ten months involve heavier wires and possibly elastics. If all goes well, the braces are removed all at one time; the teeth are thoroughly cleaned and impressions for retainers are taken. Final x-rays and photographs are also taken at this visit. In two or three days the retainers are placed in the patient's mouth, and their care and use is thoroughly explained. They are to be worn twenty-four hours per day with no exceptions until further notice. The retainers are adjusted in six weeks and then checked at three months and at six months. If all is well, the patients may be allowed to wear the retainers just at night after the initial six months of constant wear. Then the retainers are checked every six months until the wisdom teeth (third molars) have erupted normally or have been extracted. Smart patients wear their retainers at night indefinitely.

Wisdom teeth are noted for making the newly straightened teeth (especially lower front teeth) get crooked again. For this reason orthodontists frequently refer completed patients to oral surgeons to have the wisdom teeth extracted before retainers may be discontinued. In any case it is a good idea to wear the retainers as long as possible to insure the teeth stay straight. If you decide not to have the wisdom teeth removed, be absolutely certain to keep wearing those retainers to keep the teeth straight.

The Pain Factor with Braces

You can expect some pain associated with braces, but it is mild compared to most dental pain. In my practice, I never gave one patient a shot of anesthetic for any aspect of braces. We didn't even have a needle in the office. I tried to get that message across to the patients very early - "We do not give shots for braces". I think they were all glad to hear that, but it was a while before they believed me completely.

There are two kinds of orthodontic pain. The teeth themselves get sore at first when the wire puts pressure on them. In two or three days, this pressure is reduced as the teeth begin to move, and for the rest of the month the teeth move without pain. Then the appliance (braces) is adjusted and the teeth get sore again for two or three days, and it starts all over. In essence, the teeth that are adjusted (and we don't adjust all the teeth every time) are sore for two or three days every month, and only those two or three days. That means children usually eat gingerly for those three days, and then they eat normally for the rest of the month.

The second kind of orthodontic pain affects the lips. The braces tend to make the lips sore on the inside because the brackets (part of the braces that hold the wire) feel sharp to the very tender inside of the lips. Nature has a solution for this situation and the lips become slightly thickened on the inside and are tougher and more resistant to the sharpness of the brackets. Usually the lips are sore only at the beginning of treatment, unless the patient gets hit in the mouth. There is a fringe benefit here. If the patient gets hit hard enough in the mouth to knock a tooth out, the wires help prevent this from happening. I have seen many teeth knocked out of line with braces on them, but I feel sure they would have been knocked completely out without braces. Because the teeth are already loose they realign rapidly when the wires are adjusted. Even though the teeth are knocked out of line and loose, they must be brought back in place gradually. A thin wire is fastened to the teeth with plastic elastic ties so a gradual pressure acts on each tooth. In that way, they come back into place pretty easily and without much pain.

Safety in the Dental Office

Disease control in the dental office is a controversial subject. The government has given OSHA (Occupational Safety and Health Administration) oversight on how various procedures are done in all health-care situations to protect patients as well as health-care workers. OSHA's rules have changed the way the dental office looks as well as functions. All practitioners and assistants are mandated to always wear latex gloves, face masks, safety glasses, and full coverage gowns or clothing that is removed before leaving the office. It may then be laundered at the office or may be taken home to launder in some cases. All chemical items must be labeled with large labels, special colors and stored in special places out of the way of the casual visitor. The OSHA manual is a notebook about an inch thick. It is very comprehensive. OSHA inspectors have been known to drop in unannounced to inspect dental as well as medical facilities.

After the initial reluctance of dental practitioners to comply (because of the added expense of gloves, masks, gowns, washing machines, etc.), dentists have accepted and followed the rules. Since dentists might see or treat an AIDS patient, it has made universal precautions for sterility easier to accept. After 10 or so years of these procedures, OSHA has taken on a new image. Instead of the mean big brother looking over your shoulder, they are viewed as helpers and advisors to aid dental professionals in protecting their patients, their employees and themselves. That is a welcome change, at least in our perception.

The latest thing to make the headlines about hazards in the dental office is the question of water safety. Regular dental units have water lines running from city water sources to handpieces or nozzles which deliver water under pressure. Much of the water is immediately vacuumed away, but some may be swallowed or go into a wound or extraction site. Bacteria have been found in city water and therefore, dental offices, but there have been no studies showing any disease transmitted to the patient that way. The bacteria found have been of the mostly harmless variety, and luckily not something more serious. The water at the dental office is about like taking a drink of city water out of the tap at home. There are some bacteria there, but so far they have not been harmful ones

Dental equipment manufacturers are working diligently to make units capable of making sure that the water supply is sterile. In addition, dentists and their assistants clean all equipment very carefully and flush out all hoses with sterile water and a chemical cleaner. No report has ever been made of disease being accidentally transmitted to a patient in the dental office, and every dentist I know doesn't want to be the first to have it happen to his or her patient. Orthodontists use even less water under high pressure and usually don't have regular dental units. They are, however, just as concerned as general dentists to protect your and your child's health.

In my years of practicing orthodontics I never knew of a patient getting sick or injured in the dental office. I know of dentists and orthodontists who have caught illnesses from their patients. I caught innumerable colds and one case of the mumps. To us those are occupational hazards. We do, however, want to prevent our patients from catching anything from us. Our masks and gloves should help that situation. We also autoclave (moist heat sterilizer) all our instruments to be sure that germs are not spread by anything that we put in a patients mouth. A large number of offices these days even have an air purifier system in place. The air is purified and at the same time some of those wonderful smells of the dental office are removed.

Allergies may also be a concern in certain instances. Some patients are allergic to a great number of chemicals. Sometimes the adhesive we use to glue on the brackets can elicit an allergic reaction. I even had two patients who were allergic to the metal used in the orthodontic bands that we were using then. Since we rarely use bands now that is a smaller hazard. At any rate, the reactions were mild and did not require removal of the appliances. The kids allergic to the metal bands had mild swelling of lips and tongue and some gum redness. Their allergist gave them an antihistamine medication which they took before appointments and we proceeded normally. Those allergic to cements had a very mild gum irritation. It was a factor only when we were actually bonding metal brackets on teeth. Most patients didn't enjoy having their impressions taken for study models. It was not a matter of allergies; they just didn't like that tray full of soft jelly stuff in their mouths. I always told them that it looked like cake icing, but didn't taste like it. The dental supply companies have a number of different flavors for impression materials. They smell good, but the taste does not resemble the advertised flavor. In fact, most of my patients agreed that the flavored materials tasted worse than the original material. The taste and the feeling of helplessness were the worst thing about impressions, but they certainly were not injurious to the patient. I have even taken impressions of a three month old baby to help remedy the effects of her cleft palate.

Many people are concerned about the number of x-rays taken in the dental office. This field is monitored very closely by federal and state agencies. Federal agencies set the maximum number of radiographs that a dental patient can safely have every year. State agencies come to the office annually and test the x-ray machine to insure that it is doing what it is supposed to and nothing more. They even dictate lead shielding in the walls if the x-ray beam is aimed at areas where patients or staff might be sitting. They can detect any stray radiation coming from the machine and make repairs as necessary. X-ray manufacturers, like practically everyone else, are improving their machines and the speed of their x-ray film so that even less radiation is required to make a good diagnostic radiograph. The total radiation in a full mouth series of radiographs is significantly less than only 5 or 10 years ago. It has improved to the point that it isn't even very controversial anymore.

The biggest concern about dental offices is their failure to get more people to come in for checkups. This concern is for the absent people who, for whatever reason, do not take good care of their teeth. Fluoridated water has decreased the instance of cavities markedly. Many people think that is just luck. Trust me, it isn't. Fluoride in the water can't do everything. Routine checkups, cleanings and routine restorations help you keep your teeth and stay away from those major dental procedures that follow gum disease and lost teeth.

G. Ray Callahan, DDS MS

Braces for Children Ages Five through Seventeen

Chapter Three

The Concept of Early Treatment

It is very common these days to see advertisements in the newspaper advocating early treatment of children's orthodontic problems. They request bringing your child in as early as four or five years of age. Orthodontists like to intercept pending problems if they benefit the child. There's not much treatment they can do at that age, but sometimes they can help with a thumbsucking problem, but I don't recommend that until age five. At ages six, seven, and eight the orthodontist can do limited treatment, including crossbites. To correct a crossbite, an expansion appliance is cemented to the upper first molars, and the arch is widened painlessly. Nothing usually needs to be done to the lower teeth at this time. In about three or four months the appliance is removed, and usually a retainer is not needed. Another early treatment is to close the space between the upper front teeth. They erupt in a down and out direction so there should be spaces between those teeth. When the canine teeth (third from the front) come in they are angled forward, and they are supposed to move the four upper front teeth together. The canines don't erupt before ages ten or eleven, so don't worry about spaces between the front teeth until then. There is one exception to this rule: if your dentist says that the two front teeth are so far apart there is no chance the canines can move them together, I would recommend they be closed by the orthodontist. If that is necessary, the two upper front teeth should be retained with a fixed retainer glued to the inside of the front teeth, and not with a removable retainer. If a retainer should be lost, the

35

space will open up immediately, and the treatment must be done all over again. I would prefer not to treat cases in two phases (an early treatment and a later full treatment) because it usually means a longer total treatment time. However, periodontal considerations and other situations may force the orthodontist to treat that way. Some orthodontists feel extraction of permanent teeth in borderline cases can be avoided by early intervention. That was not the main reason I did some two-phase treatments. I had some patients who were taken to Europe by their parents for a year or two so I had to divide their treatment in two parts. The results were fine and everyone was happy.

Growth and Treatment Timing

Any decision as to when a child should have full orthodontic treatment should hinge on getting an ideal result in the least possible time. Of course, timing is different for girls and boys; girls mature earlier so they can be started sooner than boys.

From ten to thirteen is usually an ideal time to start treating girls. Since treatment takes two years on the average, it should be completed at least by age fifteen, a time when girls are very conscious of their appearance. They have been known to really put the pressure on the orthodontist to "Get these braces off"!

From eleven to fourteen is the normal time to start treating boys. They don't complain as much when they are nearing completion of treatment. Of course, there are exceptions to the general age range. I have seen girls and boys with a full permanent dentition by age nine. That doesn't mean I treated them at that time. Children who mature early dentally usually are not mature enough emotionally for the responsibilities of braces. Nine year old children are frequently in a non-growing stage, and treatment proceeds very slowly. When they start growing, treatment speeds up. Nine and ten-year-olds are very anxious to start treatment. They think it makes them look like teenagers. The orthodontist and the parent must be firm and treat the child when the time is ideal physiologically.

The Importance of Patient Cooperation

Cooperation is very important in orthodontic treatment. The success of a great many cases depends directly on the patient. Parents don't realize the importance of making sure their child is a good patient. Every case requires the patient, with a parent's assistance if needed, to do the following: 1. keep the teeth clean, 2. keep the braces clean, 3. wear whatever auxiliaries the doctor has prescribed, (these may be rubber bands, headgear, bite wafers, retainers, etc.), 4. keep appointments on time and 5. floss regularly.

If at all possible, parents should check their child's teeth after brushing and flossing. They need to look for rubber bands or other appliances their child is supposed to wear.

Parents should understand what the orthodontist is trying to do and reinforce these ideas with their child.

The main motivational approach in my practice was to make friends with the child while I was doing certain procedures where I didn't need any cooperation. By the time I needed the child to wear rubber bands, we were usually good enough friends that the child would do it for me. I never tried to force a patient to do anything. I frequently put forth a lot of effort to cultivate a friendship with a particularly difficult patient, and I was usually successful. If the patient doesn't cooperate with the orthodontist, then the result will be compromised, resulting in either front or back teeth that do not line up right. Orthodontists can do a lot, but the difference between great and average results is patient cooperation. I don't think most children realize the importance their own attitude plays in their successful treatment.

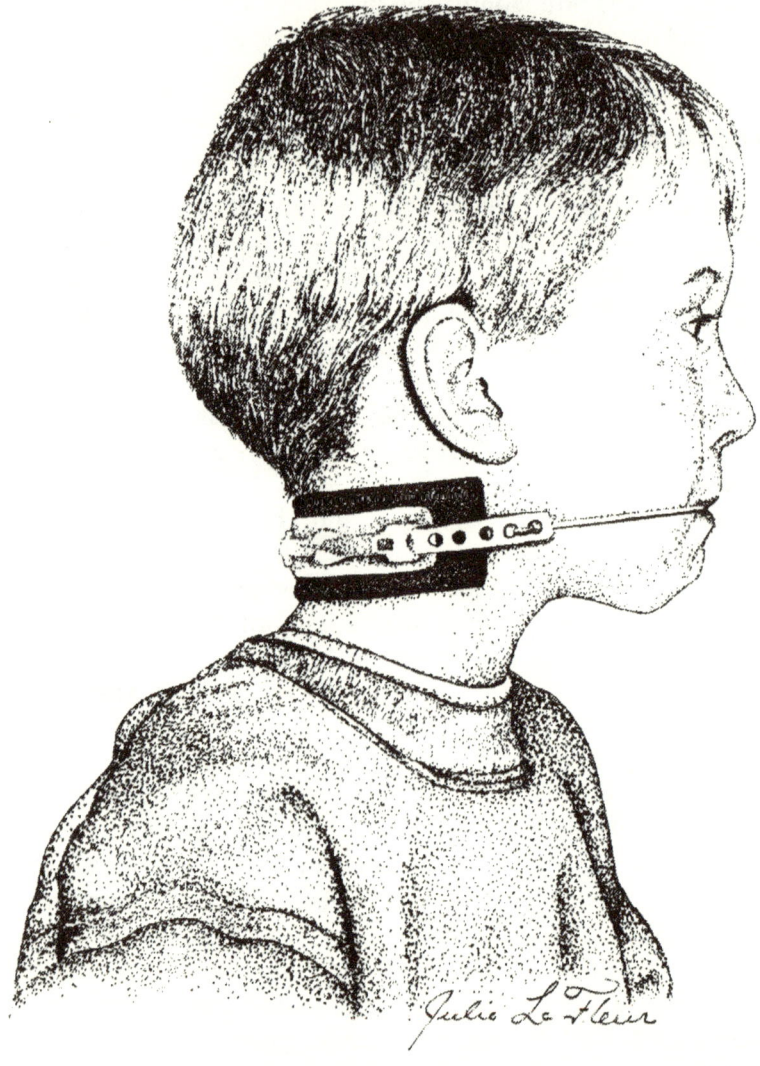

Figure 17 Low Pull Headgear.

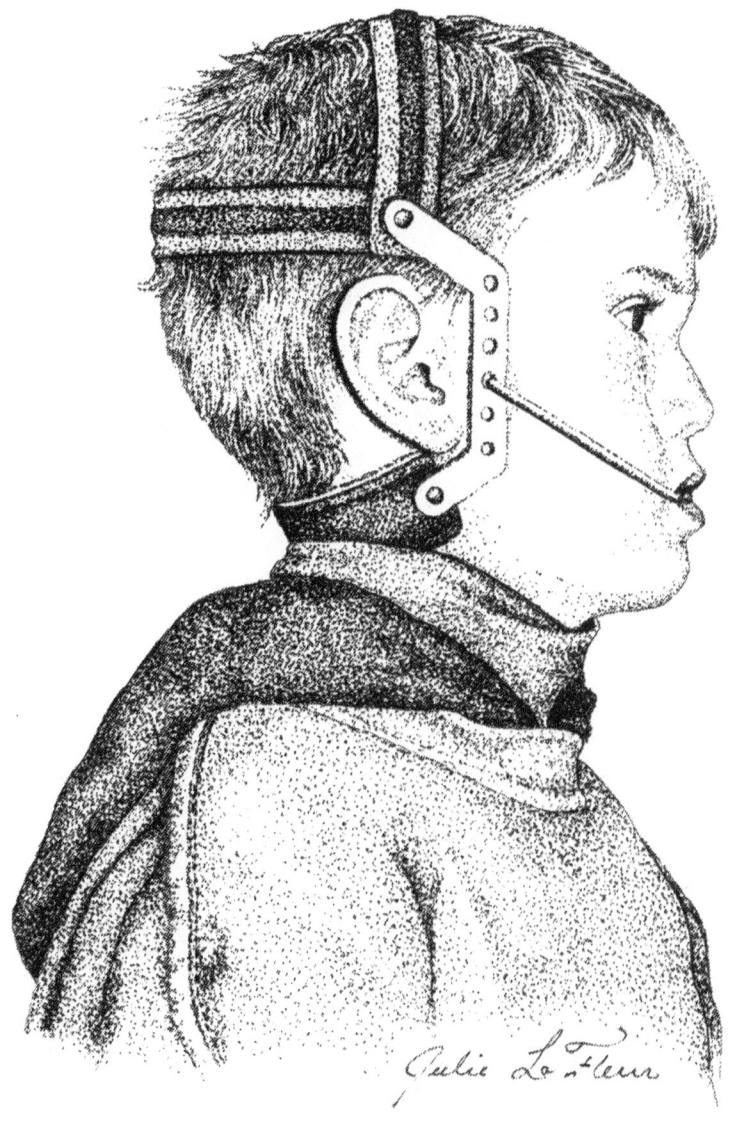

Figure 18 Directional Force Headgear (After Nola Specialties, Inc. Hilton Head Island, SC. 29925).

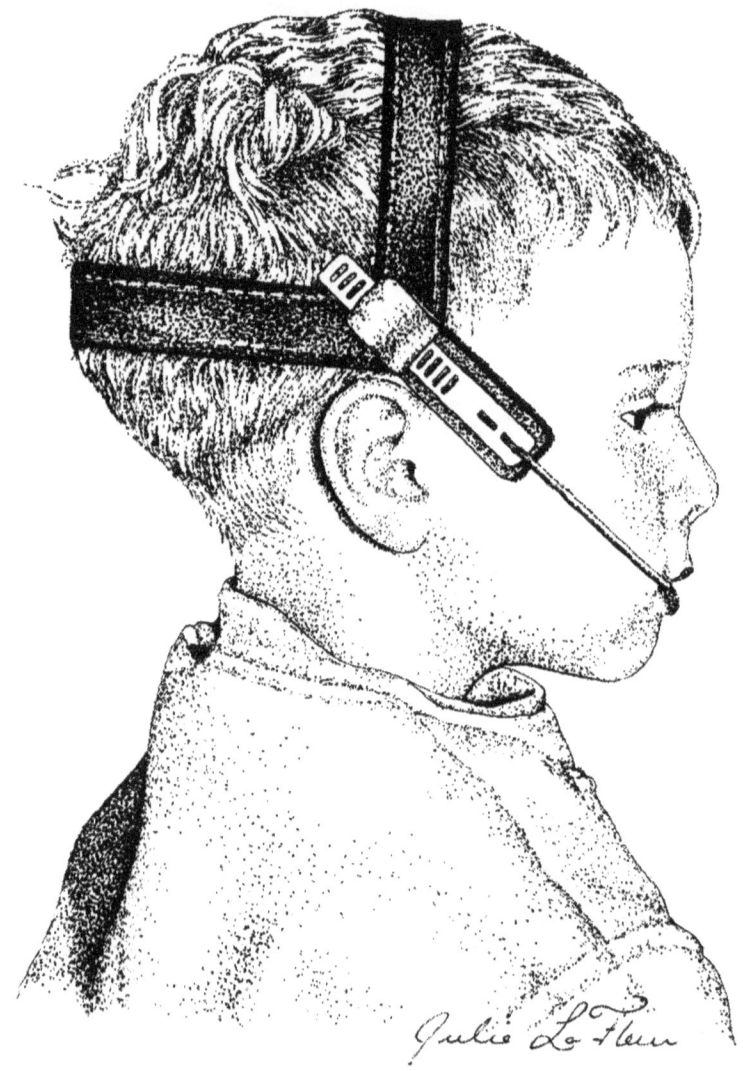

Figure 19 High Pull Headgear

Most of the tasks we ask of the patient involve getting pressure on the upper teeth in order to either move them back or hold them where they are while we move the lower teeth.

The headgear has a wire that goes into tubes on the last upper molar teeth, and an elastic band that goes around the neck. In this manner we get pressure on the upper teeth without any effect on the lower teeth.

If we also want to move the lower teeth forward elastics or rubber bands are more common but a reverse headgear may be a better method. Elastics run from the upper front teeth to the lower back teeth if we want the upper teeth to move back and the lower teeth to move forward. If they attach to the lower front teeth and the upper back teeth, the lower teeth come back and the upper teeth come forward. If the lower teeth need to be moved forward without moving the upper teeth at all, the reverse headgear does the job. The real problem here is that if the patient does not wear the headgear or elastics as the orthodontist recommends, the proposed movement does not take place. The doctor has very few ways to make these movements happen without the patient wearing these auxiliaries. Most patients and parents don't fully realize that patient cooperation is critical to good results.

Thumbsucking and Other Habits

Thumbsucking is very common in our lifestyle. If the average child stops completely before the age of five, whatever trouble they have caused the teeth should be self-correcting. If the child sucks the thumb constantly day and night, the teeth will be affected. The front teeth won't come together when the back teeth are touching solidly. This creates an anterior open bite. When the child eventually stops sucking the thumb, the tongue will come into this space to close it off so that the child can swallow. This is called a "tongue thrust."

41

G. Ray Callahan, DDS MS

It is quite common to be able to tell which thumb the patient actually sucks. Parents and patients alike are impressed when the orthodontist mentions that the patient sucks the right or left thumb. The teeth are held apart on the side of the favorite thumb much more than the other side. You can frequently see the exact hole between the teeth where the thumb goes. Orthodontists have a standard procedure to correct thumb habits. Sometimes they cement an appliance in the mouth, and other times the verbal approach works. About ninety percent of the time they are successful. The other ten percent are usually referred out to speech pathologists or myofunctional therapists. These techniques are time consuming and not cheap, but they are very important. Straightening the teeth in the face of a severe tongue habit is looking failure right in the eye.

Figure 20 Five year olds demonstrating thumbsucking.

Figure 21 Pacifier use should stop around two years old.

The patient may have to have permanent retention after orthodontic treatment if the habit is still active. It is a lot simpler if you encourage your child to use a pacifier. If the child can get used to a pacifier, it will be a source of great peace in the household for the child and parent alike. The secret, however, is to make sure the pacifier does a disappearing act between ages one and two. Four and five year olds walking around with a pacifier in their mouths will have the same problems as the severe thumbsucker - open bite malocclusion and a tongue thrust swallowing habit. Both of those are expensive to correct.

One of my patients had a solution of her own. She fell off her bicycle and broke both forearms. The accident was unfortunate, but it sure fixed her thumbsucking habit.

While we're on the subject of habits, fingernail biting can be irritating and painful. Fortunately, orthodontic treatment frequently solves this problem without even trying. The braces make the front teeth sore at certain times, and even prevent contact with lower teeth for a while - making nail biting tough to accomplish. By the time the treatment is finished, the nail biting habit is often over.

Habits are a constant problem for orthodontists. Thumbsucking can be dealt with fairly easily but some of the others are more difficult, like tongue sucking. Many young children don't necessarily use their thumbs or pacifiers, yet they end up sucking their tongues when they are tired or bored. It frequently causes an anterior open bite.

Sometimes the bite may be open on the right or left side also. Treatment involves placing sharp wires on the inside tooth surfaces to keep the tongue in place. Usually nothing is done until braces are in place when it is easier to control the tongue. Retention must be observed very carefully to keep the bite from opening up again. With proper motivation of the patient, a tooth positioner works well in this situation.

Some patients make a habit of lip biting which results in frequent unsightly sores on the lips. This habit usually arises from crooked teeth that bite the lip easily. When the teeth are straightened it is not so easy and the habit usually stops. Constant pressure on the face or jaws from postural positioning of hands or arms may cause some facial change. In most cases, merely bringing it to the patient's attention may correct the problem.

School, Athletics and Appointments

Orthodontic appointments average a four to eight week interval. They can be scheduled at the same day and time or they can be varied so that the same class isn't missed every time. The appointments usually last fifteen to twenty minutes, so the school time lost is not very much. We had a standard school excuse form which the doctor signed and gave to the patient to take back to school. With this kind of system, we never had trouble with the schools over our appointments. Occasionally a teenager would take the day off after our appointment, and blame it on us, but if the teacher called, the jig was up. We had many patients from nearby small towns who carpooled to our office. It saved a lot of transportation money.

We always encouraged our patients to participate in athletics, and other extracurricular activities such as band and theatre. All the contact sports required mouthpieces to be worn to protect the lips and teeth from damage. Braces are a little difficult for musicians, especially brass players, but sore lips can be overcome by a little extra wax over the sharp spots. We also recommended that patients in non-contact sports wear a mouthpiece to avoid making their lips sore. Perceived hazards of two patients kissing and getting their braces hooked together are vastly overrated. It never happened to my patients in my years of practice. I did have two patients marry who met in my waiting room. With great pleasure I also treated their two children about twelve years later.

G. Ray Callahan, DDS MS

Chapter Four

Cleft Palate Treatment

Cleft palate is a relatively common birth defect. It occurs in approximately 1 in 600 births. It results from two embryological processes not fusing together as normally happens. This failure to fuse leaves an opening through the upper jaw on one side of the midline, or on both sides. It can be very severe and affect the whole upper jaw or it can be only a little mark on the lip. Complete unilateral or bilateral clefts have to be surgically repaired while the child is small. The treatment of choice today involves the orthodontist and the surgeon immediately after birth[2]. After only a few weeks the orthodontist makes an acrylic (plastic) palate fitted to the roof of the mouth so the child can suck better. At about two months the surgeon repairs the lip. The lip pressure and the appliance guide the two bony ridges separated by the cleft into alignment and the surgeon places a bone graft to stabilize the bony ridges[3]. The entire palate is then closed at about one year of age.

Large metropolitan areas have large hospitals that also usually have teams of doctors who take care of severe facial deformities. These doctors represent all the specialties who normally are involved in cleft palate treatment. At the very least such treatment includes a general medical practitioner, a

---

[2] Sheldon W. Rosenstein, DDS, MSD, "Two unilateral complete cleft lip and palate orthodontic cases treated from birth to adolescence," *American Journal of Orthodontics and Dentofacial Orthopedics,* CXV (January 1999), 61-71.
[3] Dado, D.V. Early primary bone-grafting. In: Kernahan, D.A, Rosenstein SW, editors. Cleft lip and palate: a system of management. Baltimore: Williams & Wilkins; 1990. p.120-7.

pediatrician, an oral surgeon, a plastic surgeon, a general dentist, an orthodontist, a psychologist, a social worker, an audiologist and a dental hygienist. I served on a team with all these specialties for over 20 years. All of these people worked without fee so we could plan treatment for any patient needing this care.

Clefts occur in the area of the upper lateral incisors so those teeth are affected greatly. Frequently they are missing. If they are present they are usually malpositioned or severely rotated. The teeth usually look so bad that the parents are very anxious for the orthodontist to get busy. Between ages seven and eight the orthodontist can usually correct crossbites and severe rotations. Usually it is better for the patient if the orthodontist can wait until the normal age to do much full treatment. Most orthodontists will move the front teeth as quickly as possible and then get the braces off until the patients get older and more teeth erupt. Of course that means that the patient must wear a retainer for several years until they are ready for full treatment. If the retainers are lost or not worn or broken then the teeth move apart and it must be done over again. It can be very frustrating.

If the patient can have full treatment when most of the permanent teeth are in place, a better result can be obtained. Bone grafts which are placed in the area of the cleft allow a lateral incisor to actually be moved into that bone. If the lateral is well formed it is completely normal in the new bone. If the lateral incisor is actually missing it will first be replaced by a false tooth tied into the braces which looks very good. When braces are removed a false tooth will be placed on the retainer which also looks very good. When the retainer would normally be discontinued, I always cut the wire off the front of the plastic palate and left it there to hold the artificial tooth. In that way the tooth was in place, but no wires gave away the fact that it was fake. Eventually the patient can have a fixed bridge to replace the missing tooth which will hopefully last for a lifetime.

A cleft patient commonly has a series of cosmetic surgeries to correct the lip and nose deformity. Oral surgeons and plastic surgeons can only make facial revisions at certain stages of the patient's development. It is important to have the teeth properly aligned before final lip surgeries. If more than one or two teeth are missing, which is pretty common in these cases, it may be necessary to have a partial denture made. That is usually only used for a short time because it must be kept absolutely clean or it will destroy the remaining teeth. Young patients have a hard time doing that so we try to avoid it. Now an implant is often placed and a crown attached to it.

Extraction or Non-extraction?

In other words, extraction means "pulling or removing teeth". Sometimes when the orthodontist gets all his records together, measures everything he can, and puts it all together into a diagnosis, it doesn't work out right. Then the orthodontist must determine what he or she needs to do to make sure everything does work out. Teeth have been measured in every way imaginable since orthodontics became a specialty. Not only their widths have been measured, but also the angle with which they relate to other anatomical normals, and their relative positions in the arch.

While all orthodontists would prefer not to extract teeth to accomplish a satisfactory result, there is one thing all orthodontists prefer more than removing teeth: a successful result. Success means the teeth are straight; they look good; they function normally, and they are stable. Anytime the orthodontist goes through a good diagnosis and there is too much tooth material present or the teeth are in some radical position, some of it must be removed. The amount or number of teeth to be removed can be determined by the diagnosis. Many times a set of crowded teeth, which look impossible to straighten without extractions, can be successfully done nonextraction. In fact, they must be done nonextraction for an ideal result.

Luckily for us all, some early orthodontists appreciated the value of an accurate diagnosis before beginning treatment. One such scientist was Dr. W. A. Bolton[4] who measured thousands of teeth and developed relationship formulas to determine how wide the six upper front teeth should be to properly relate to the six lower front teeth. He also did the same for the whole arch and for the posterior segments. Even today accurate diagnosis demands that the orthodontist measure all the teeth to determine their relationship. A few years later another noted, early orthodontist, named Dr. Charles Tweed[5] took this a step further by analyzing how the teeth related to the lips and face. His contention was that even though the teeth were straight and in the proper relationship to each other, if they made the face look bad, they weren't right. He also proved that they wouldn't stay straight unless they were properly related to the bony structures of the face. Cephalometric radiographs (head x-rays) which are available to everyone these days, have made these analyses routine. The orthodontist can determine exactly what moving the teeth to a given location will do to the facial appearance and evaluate closely what the stability will be in that position.

Now you know why the orthodontist needs all those records, radiographs and study models. If your child does need extractions, you can be assured the orthodontist has done the diagnosis and determined the best treatment. Sometimes the spaces left after some teeth have been removed look awfully big, but the orthodontist needs that space to get the teeth into their proper positions. The space will all be gone when the case is finished or it isn't finished.

---

[4] Dr. W. A. Bolton, "Disharmony in tooth size and its relation to the analysis and treatment of malocclusion," *Angle Orthodontist*, XXVIII (1958), 113-130.
[5] Dr. Charles H. Tweed, "A Philosophy of orthodontic treatment," *American Journal of Orthodontics and Oral Surgery,* (February, 1945).

Braces and Faces

Many people don't realize that the lower face (lips and chin) is greatly affected by the position of the front teeth. Prominent lips attributed to inherited family traits may be just a sign that the same crooked teeth are causing the problem. This presents a tricky situation for the orthodontist. Parents may not want to hear that their child's face isn't the way the orthodontist feels it should be. I always tried not to bring up the subject of facial appearance at the initial examination. Basically I talked about the teeth. When I had a tracing of the cephalometric radiograph at the consultation appointment, I would say, "Oh, by the way, moving these teeth will also make the lips move too". I would draw in on the tracing a new lip profile, and wait for the parent to observe that it looked better. If they didn't talk about it, I didn't either. Most people don't come in with a complaint about lip posture because they have been looking at their child for eleven or twelve years, and they love them the way they are. Fortunately, though, crooked teeth give us an opportunity to also improve the lip profile. Lip posture and facial profile are affected by genetics as well as ethnic background. A profile acceptable in one geographic area might be unattractive in another. Orthodontists do their best to attain the results the patient or parent desires.

Sometimes the facial profile can be improved by a surgical procedure such as chin augmentation or reduction (making it larger or smaller). It is a simple operation, but must be performed by an oral surgeon. It can sometimes be done in the surgeon's office under local anesthesia. For many reasons it is probably more commonly done in a hospital setting so general anesthesia can be used.

Any discussion of profile improvement must include the surgery that can reshape the nose or enlarge or reduce various parts of the face. Oral surgeons and physicians who are plastic surgeons can do wondrous changes to the face. These

51

procedures are almost always done in a hospital and are usually covered by insurance.

Functional Appliances

Other appliances, besides braces, used to correct crooked teeth are called "Functional Appliances". They are removable appliances used mainly in Europe as opposed to the fixed appliances used mainly in the United States. A certain number of doctors in the United States also use the functional appliances. These appliances are fairly large retainer-type devices with more wire springs than retainers and more plastic area. Functional appliances are used extensively in Europe because one doctor with auxiliary help can treat many more patients than the average orthodontist in the United States using fixed appliances. Of course, this may be due to the greater number of orthodontists in the United States than in Europe. European orthodontists don't use only functional appliances, and their results seem to be on a par with ours so their motivational skills must be good.

Functional appliances are worn for a long period of time, maybe five or six years and are designed to expand the upper back teeth and reposition the whole lower jaw forward. In this way they correct the type of malocclusion where the upper teeth stick out ahead of the lower jaw. Again the secret here is a motivated patient willing to wear the appliance for twenty-four hours per day. Anything less will result in failure. Abnormal muscular habits, such as thumb sucking, tongue pressure, etc., may upset the delicate balance between teeth and musculature in the mouth.

With a high percentage of malocclusions related to musculature it is apparent why functional appliances are used so often. Many more patients can be treated this way because the average cost of functional appliances is less than fixed appliances. The reason for this is the laboratory person constructs the functional appliance outside the mouth, rather than the doctor doing it inside the mouth.

Functional appliances have many designs. They are usually named after their method of action or the orthodontist who designed them. Each country seems to have their favorite practitioner who made a certain type of appliance and his followers in that area usually use it. One type of functional appliance is the twin block.

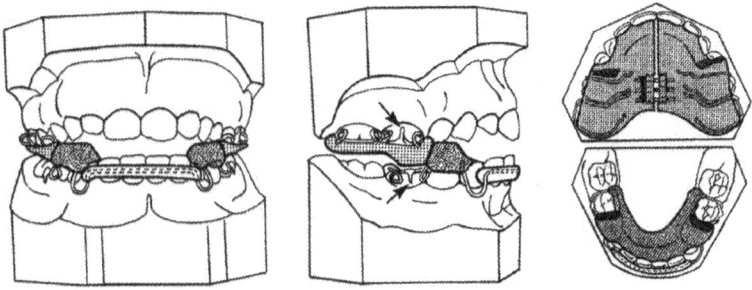

Modified Twin Block design (after Mills and McCulloch, AJODO, July, 2000,p.25)

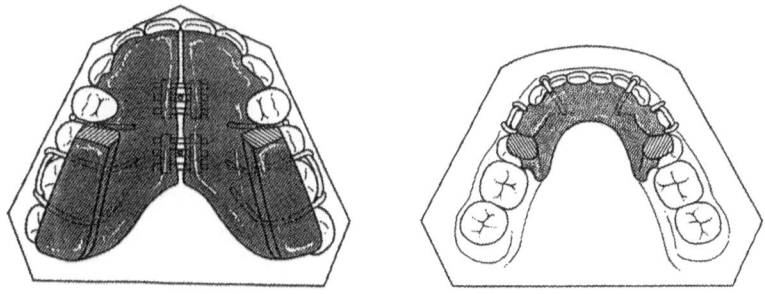

Figure 22 Twin Block Functional Appliance (after Toth and McNamara, AJODO, Dec. 1999)

G. Ray Callahan, DDS MS

Braces for Adults Over Age Eighteen

Chapter Five

Adult Orthodontics

Parents and other adults are candidates for orthodontic treatment just like their children. Their treatment is just as successful and frequently doesn't take any longer to do. When parents brought in their children for treatment, I always offered to do their treatment at the same time if I could see at a glance that either or both of them had a problem. It was amazing to me how many agreed. Of course, they had always wanted to have the treatment, but were afraid they were too old. I was a little surprised at first how successful it really was to treat adults. They are wonderful patients, because they are there for results, not social acceptance. Braces can be done at any age, and if everything in the mouth is healthy, it proceeds normally. People with periodontal (gum) problems had to be cleared for treatment with a periodontist before we would treat them in my office.

Adults frequently are interested in limited orthodontic treatment for localized problems. In other words they may want a space closed, a crooked tooth aligned or spaces adjusted prior to bridgework by their general dentist. All of these procedures are possible and the orthodontist is glad to do them if there is a reasonable chance for success. Many limited procedures require permanent retention for stability. Adult patients are very interested in tooth colored braces because they don't attract so much attention. The latest ceramic brackets are very similar to tooth enamel and are almost invisible from three feet away. Ceramic brackets cost a little more, but do the same job as metal brackets and look better at the same time. A number of adults were also interested in lingual braces (appliance attached to the inside of upper and lower teeth) because they didn't show

55

anything to the casual observer. Cost is a factor with lingual braces so they are not normally marketed to teenagers. I always felt that parents would object to encouraging their child to want an appliance that cost twice as much as the regular one.

Current Facts and Fads about Braces

The basic part of braces is the bracket. The bracket is glued to each tooth in the mouth. Each bracket has a slot that holds a wire. Ultimately it is the wire that moves the tooth. The type of bracket used is determined by the type of appliance (the system of braces) that each doctor uses. Probably the oldest appliance in use today is the Edgewise Appliance, which was invented by Dr. Edward H. Angle[6], the father of modern orthodontics.

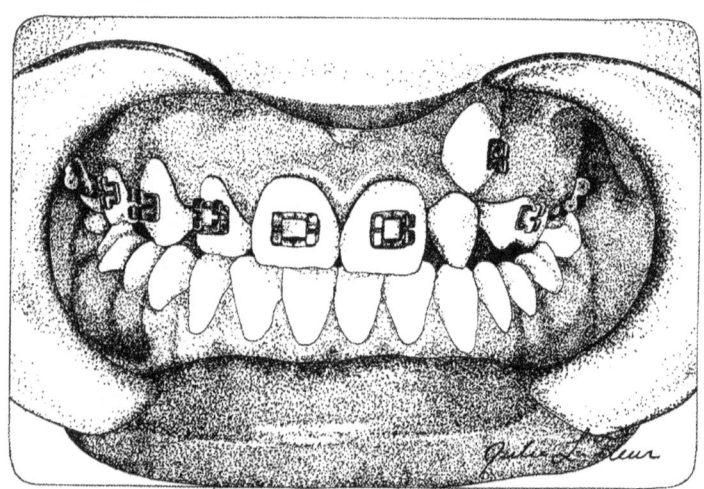

Figure 23 Edgewise brackets on teeth without wires in place.

---

[6] Angle, E.H. Treatment of Malocclusion of the Teeth. Angle System. Philadelphia. S.S. White;1907. P.60-87.

He developed a bracket that featured a precisely tooled slot which measured 0.022 x 0.028 inches in size. Earlier, and now obsolete, appliances had placed the longer side of a rectangular wire against the tooth. Dr. Angle designed his appliance with the rectangular wire going into the bracket edge first. Therefore the appliance was known as the Edgewise Appliance. It provided greater control over the teeth being moved and allowed better results in cases where teeth had to be extracted. The Edgewise Appliance is considered the best and most demanding for the doctor to master, so it is the technique taught in almost all of the orthodontic colleges. Other appliances are used in orthodontics, but they are learned after the Edgewise Technique. The most popular of the other appliances is used by about fifteen per cent of doctors. Smaller groups of doctors use a few other appliances. The advantage of virtually all orthodontists being trained with the Edgewise Technique is that if transfer cases come in everyone can treat the Edgewise cases whereas other appliances will have to be referred to someone who uses that technique.

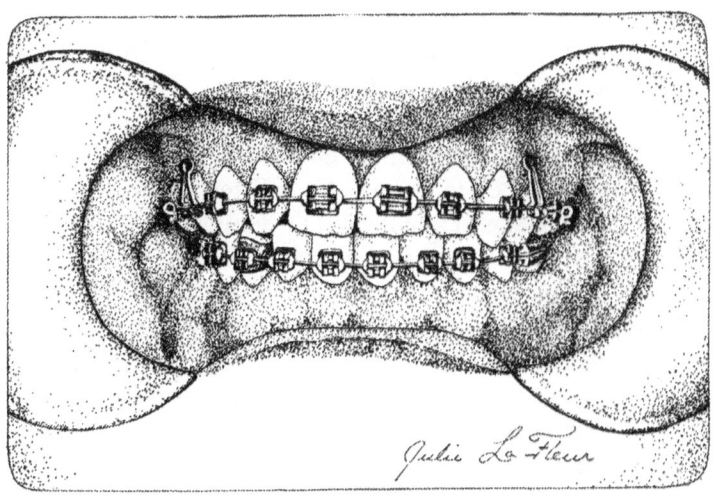

Figure 24 Edgewise appliance in place including archwires

Brackets come in many varieties. Whether square, round, rectangular, circular or triangular, they must be attached to the teeth. Again, many options exist. Most bracket placements follow a standard format: thoroughly cleaning the tooth, etching the tooth enamel with a weak acidic solution (does not damage the tooth), drying the surface completely, placing the liquid part of the adhesive on the surface of the tooth, placing the paste part of the adhesive on the base of the bracket, and positioning the bracket in the ideal spot on the tooth. Many adhesives are cured by light so a high intensity light is held on each tooth for thirty to sixty seconds. This whole procedure may be done indirectly by positioning the brackets on a precise stone model of the teeth, taking an impression with a stable impression material, then removing the impression with the brackets imbedded in it. Then the teeth are cleaned, etched, dried, and coated with part one of the adhesive. The paste is put on the backs of all brackets in the impression that is placed in the mouth and allowed to set until the adhesive is firm. The impression is easily removed and the brackets remain on the teeth. All brackets are cemented at one time so discomfort to the patient is minimal. Wires are then placed in the brackets and teeth start moving. This procedure is painless to the patient because all the patient has to do is hold their mouth open enough to allow the orthodontist to work there.

The whole procedure takes about fifteen minutes. Usually the doctor does one arch at a time. The doctor wants to minimize a patient's discomfort and prevent reluctance to return for the next appointment. All orthodontists want to make friends with their patients so too much pain is a no-no. We depend on the patient to do various tasks for us such as wearing elastics, headgear, retainers; consequently we make sure the pain doesn't become a negative factor.

Many different ways have been tried to make braces more attractive to patients, especially teenagers. Braces are made up of brackets, bands and wire. A bracket is merely a handle on the tooth so that we can put a gentle pressure on it to make it move. Brackets can be seen so they come in subtle colors such as tooth color, clear, silver and even gold. Wires also come in colors and are either round, square or rectangular in cross section. Bands are usually only on the molars and they are silver. Tooth colored and clear brackets are made of ceramics or plastic so they are more prone to breakage. Metal brackets rarely break. Any bracket, however, could come loose and have to be replaced.

Orthognathic Surgery

Orthognathic is a big word meaning straight jaws. You all know what surgery means. Crooked teeth and jaws may be beyond the orthodontist to correct alone. When the upper or lower jaw is much larger or smaller than its opposing jaw, the orthodontist can't solve the problem. However, working with an oral surgeon, a successful result can be obtained. Probably the most common example of this problem is the "bulldog" type jaw with the lower front teeth outside the upper front teeth. These cases used to be very difficult, but now we solve them regularly.

If your child or one of his or her parents has a severe bite problem, you still need to start with the orthodontist. They are well equipped to get the necessary records, and diagnose the case. If oral surgery is necessary the orthodontist will know when to refer you to an oral surgeon. They will then work together, because the orthodontist needs to put the teeth into a position where they will fit together correctly before the oral surgeon moves one or both jaws.

It sounds serious to even consider jaw surgery. It is serious, but not like living all your life with a deformed jaw. Your child might suffer all his or her life when a two hour surgical experience could solve that problem. I always tried to look at my recommendations for treatment like I was treating my own child. I definitely would have done it surgically if my children had needed it. Luckily, they didn't need it. My partner's daughter, however, did need the surgery, and she had it after both of us diagnosed her problem and her solution the same way. She came through it perfectly, and her occlusion is ideal.

In my thirty-five years of practice, averaging about twelve surgical cases per year, I never saw a surgery case that wasn't markedly improved. Some were better than others, but they all were worth doing, and the patients were happy afterward. It is a procedure which has become routine and can benefit a great many people. Surgical techniques have improved markedly over the years. I used to go to the operating room with the oral surgeon and we expected to spend four to six hours on the case. Now two hours is longer than normal for these procedures. Maybe the fact that the orthodontists don't go along has speeded up the operation.

TMJ – What Is It?

TMJ is an abbreviation for the temporomandibular joint. By definition it is where the mandible (lower jaw) contacts the temporal bones at the base of the skull. It may also be known as the jaw joint. The TMJ is important in this discussion because it may be irritated or damaged by the positions forced upon it by the poorly positioned teeth. The TMJ should be in harmony if the teeth fit together properly. Many adults and even teenagers suffer severely from TMJ pain because the crooked teeth cause interferences when biting which cause the lower jaw to move out of its ideal position. If it is forced into a backward position, it may cause clicking, pain, headaches, etc. Fortunately, these conditions can be treated very adequately, and a solution should be sought as early as possible. Your orthodontist should either be able to do the treatment or refer you to another doctor who does specialize in TMJ cases. The TMJ in children under thirteen is usually free of pain or clicking, but not always.

My youngest patient with clicking jaw joints and joint pain was nine years old. I probably saw less than ten pre-teens with TMJ problems in my years of practice.

As a child matures, the bone around the joint matures, and they may develop TMJ symptoms. The first sign of a problem is clicking in the joint (which is right in front of your ear). It isn't always a serious problem, and some people have some clicking throughout life. When children's joints start clicking around thirteen, they usually start having pain in a year or two. The symptoms are much more common in young ladies. Treatment options include braces, splints, equilibration (selective spot grinding of premature contacts on the teeth), and sometimes surgery (rarely). Always do the simplest treatment first. Many of these cases respond to mild, symptomatic type treatments. Usually a splint for several months will bring complete relief.

The orthodontist enters this TMJ treatment because many times it is necessary to align crooked teeth that are producing an interference in chewing actions. In some circumstances this can also be done with a splint. A splint is a plastic wafer custom made to guide the jaws to the proper position to not stress the TMJ. If the teeth have a very mild interference, it may be possible to correct it by grinding the offending area of tooth enamel. This is called equilibration. It is also limited by the amount of tooth structure that needs to be removed. If it exceeds the amount of tooth structure necessary for the health of the tooth, this procedure is not indicated.

Splints are very good at relieving TMJ pain, but then patients are left with the splint. They don't last forever, and they are hard to keep clean in the mouth. In my personal practice I was continually amazed at how frequently the patients called in after six months or a year and said they had lost or broken the splint. They also reported no symptoms. I always told them to keep up the good work and call me only if the symptoms came back. At this stage, if severe symptoms come back, the orthodontist may straighten the teeth to eliminate the need for the splint. It is a more permanent solution to the problem. I personally didn't want to use braces on these patients on the outside chance that my treatment would not correct the problem. Mercifully, it almost always was successful and the patients were happy with straight teeth that didn't cause TMJ symptoms. When you do a specific treatment for a specific problem, you'd better have a patient that understands that you cannot work miracles. In my office that department was handled by a Higher Authority.

The Invisalign System[7]

One of the latest developments in adult orthodontics is the Invisalign System. This is a series of clear orthodontic devices, called aligners, that allow you to straighten your teeth without having to wear traditional braces. Each set of custom-made aligners is worn for about two weeks and moves the teeth in small steps to the desired final position, as determined by you and your orthodontist. The aligners are removable for eating and brushing and flossing your teeth. They are also comfortable to wear because there are no wires, metal or permanent fixtures.

As with traditional braces, there may be some temporary minor discomfort at the beginning of each stage of treatment. This is often described as a feeling of pressure. Aligners should be worn all day, except when eating and brushing and flossing your teeth. The vast majority of patients report no effect on speech. The duration of treatment depends on the complexity of the case and is generally equal to that of traditional braces. The interval between appointments is generally the same as with traditional braces. As with regular braces, the cost of this system depends on the complexity of your case and your course of treatment decided on by you and the doctor.

Not nearly every orthodontic problem can be corrected this way. Case selection is very critical. In most cases adolescents are not eligible. This is because jaw growth must be complete and all adult teeth must be fully erupted. In addition correctable

---

[7] Invisalign © Align Technology, Inc., 442 Potrero Avenue, Sunnyvale, CA 94086

problems are mild spacing (1-3mm), moderate spacing (4-6mm), mild crowding (1-3mm), moderate crowding (4-6mm),narrow arches (dental), (4-6mm) and some relapse cases if they fit these criteria.

How is all this done? It sounds like magic. For most of us computer technology is magic. In this case the procedure starts with a complete orthodontic diagnosis involving full records and treatment plan. If the orthodontist determines that this case fits the diagnostic requirements another impression is taken of the teeth. It is a very precise and "perfect" impression made with material that does not distort with time. This impression is sent to Align Technology Inc. where a plaster model is made and analyzed by computer. The computer makes a three dimensional image which Align Technology uses to construct a "test aligner". The test aligner is immediately sent back to the orthodontist to have a trial fit in the patient's mouth. If the orthodontist finds that the test aligner fits the patient, he immediately calls Align Technology and they use their computer to start changing the teeth on their 3-D image. At predetermined intervals the technology produces a set of (upper and lower) aligners. The process moves the teeth gradually to the predetermined goal. In most cases there will be a large number of the aligners.

The aligners are worn for two weeks each and then replaced. In this way the movement increments are small and don't cause much pain. Each set of aligners brings the teeth closer to the desired goal. The last set of aligners is used when the teeth are perfect. They may be used as retainers or conventional retainers may be constructed. The period of retention should be the same as for regular braces

Lingual Braces

Lingual refers to the tongue-side of the teeth. In other words, lingual braces are put on the inside or tongue side of the teeth.

63

That means they are essentially "invisible". Of course you can see them, but you have to look at the inside surface of the teeth to see them. Lingual braces are popular with adults and young adults who are sensitive about people seeing their braces. Most of these people would not have the treatment if they had to wear the regular braces that everyone could see.

Some limitations exist on the type of cases that can be treated adequately with lingual braces. Very severe types of malocclusions and some that might require surgery are frequently too difficult for this technique, unless the orthodontist does it all the time. Treating even a routine case with lingual braces is more difficult because it requires more dexterity by the orthodontist to work in a much smaller space (inside the teeth).

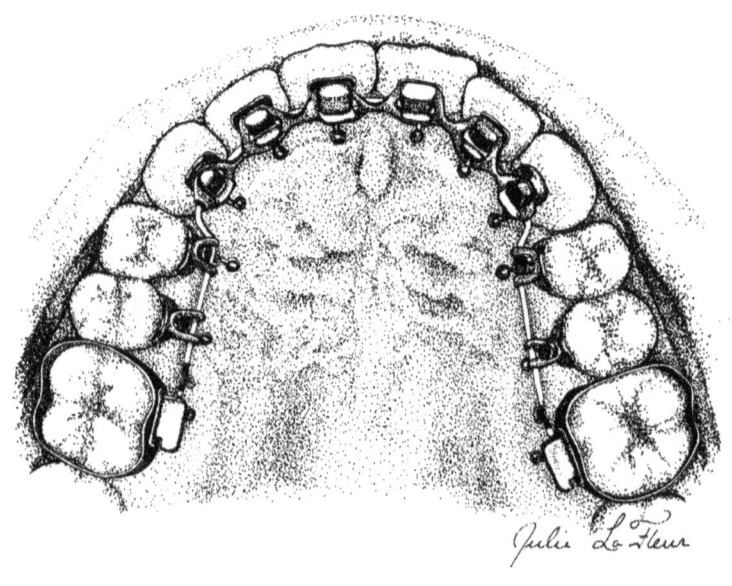

Figure 25 Lingual braces on the inside of the upper teeth.

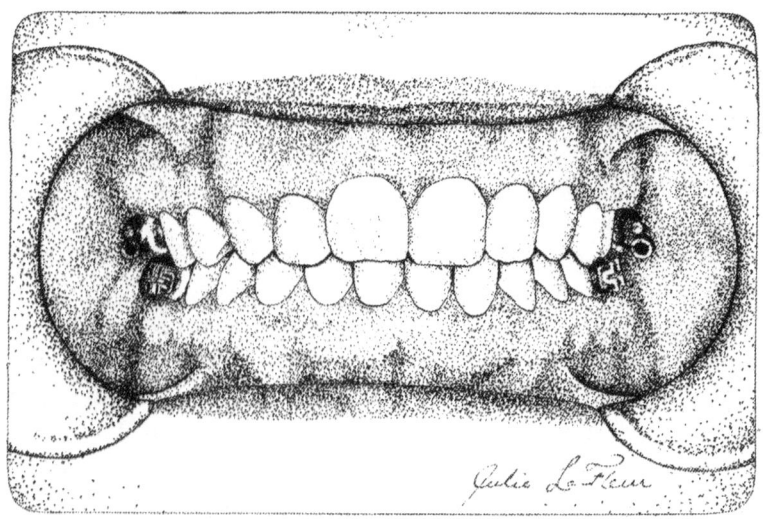

Figure 26 Lingual braces, front view.

Obviously the technique is different and essentially opposite to that used on the outside of the teeth. Since it is more difficult and takes more time with the patient, it must cost more. This becomes a limiting factor for many people. The average parent is not going to pay two or three times the regular fee for a teenager who wants to say they have invisible braces. Most people who opt for lingual braces are young, self-supporting adults who pay for their own treatment.

Surprisingly the lingual braces do not cause a significantly greater amount of pain than regular braces. My patients usually complained about a sore tongue for one to two weeks and then it was over. They didn't complain at all after that period. Lingual patients also didn't have the periodic sore lips like the people in regular braces. I found that my patients in lingual braces required a longer treatment time than necessary because they didn't keep their appointments as often as regular patients. Since no one could see their braces and their teeth were not sore, they were casual about their appointments. I had two young male patients who came in only about twice or three times a year. Needless-to-say their treatment took almost five years. It was more frustrating for me than for them.

Orthodontists who treat only lingual cases are much more efficient than I was because my lingual cases represented only about five percent of my total patients. It was, therefore, a constant mental battle to be sure I made the correct bends in my wires. On rare occasions I made the wrong bend and moved the tooth in the wrong direction and then had to reverse it the next month to get the tooth going in the right direction. I didn't make that mistake very many times because it required extra work and wrecked my schedule. I was always surprised that patients did not have sore tongues after the first two weeks. The tongue must be very adaptable to get along so well under those conditions.

Treatment Motivation Survey[8]

The treatment motivation survey gives a patient three areas to register motivation or expectations for treatment: (1) desired dental changes, (2) desired facial changes, and (3) desired symptom changes. This form clarifies the patient's treatment objectives so the doctor and patient can be in complete agreement. Please help us understand your problem by checking the following information; please be specific. (Circle words more, less, etc.)

---

[8] Treatment Motivation Survey: Defining patient motivation for treatment. By G. William Arnett, DDS, FACD, and C. MacDonald Worley, Jr., DMD, MD, BS. Copyright 1999 by the American Association of Orthodontists.

Teeth

If your teeth could be changed, how would you like them to change?

[ ] Straighten the front teeth upper/lower

[ ] Straighten the back teeth upper/lower

[ ] Make the upper front teeth longer/shorter

[ ] Move upper teeth forward/backward

[ ] Move lower teeth forward/backward

[ ] Make the line of the upper front teeth level
    forward/backward

[ ] Move the midline of the upper/lower teeth to the right/left

[ ] Other_____

Face

If your facial appearance could be changed, what would you change?

[ ] Get rid of sag under lower jaw

[ ] Move chin forward/backward

[ ] Move chin left/right to center it

67

[ ] Move lower lip forward/backward

[ ] Move upper lip forward/backward

[ ] Move the area around my nose forward/backward

[ ] Move the area under my eyes forward/backward

[ ] Make the profile of my nose forward/backward

[ ] Make my cheekbones larger/smaller

[ ] Show more/less of my teeth/gums when I smile

[ ] Make my lips closer together/farther apart when my teeth are touching

[ ] Make my lips not touch and roll out when my teeth are touching

[ ] Reduce the strain in my chin/lips when I close my lips

[ ] Make my face more narrow/wide

[ ] Reduce the width/fullness of my lower jaw behind my mouth

[ ] Other_____

Symptoms

If you want to reduce pain or discomfort where would it be located? Please be specific about the location: circle the right side, left side or both if they apply.

[ ] In front of my ears right/left

[ ] Below my ears right/left

[ ] Above my ears right/left

[ ] In my ears right/left

[ ] Neck right/left

[ ] Shoulders right/left

[ ] Temples right/left

[ ] Teeth

[ ] Sinuses

[ ] Eyes right/left

[ ] Other_____

G. Ray Callahan, DDS MS

Forms You Might Need To Sign

Chapter Six

In any orthodontic office you will be given various forms to read and fill out. The first will be a health history. You should be able to do it easily without having to call your medical doctor for information. The next form will not come until after records have been taken and you have decided to go ahead with treatment. There are actually two forms that usually come at the same time. One is an informed consent document stating all possible complications of the treatment, no matter how remote. Patient and parent should both read this form because both are expected to sign it. The other document is a combined truth-in-lending and installment contract form stating exactly how much the treatment costs, how you are expected to pay it, and what the interest is if you don't pay it on time. These forms vary, but everyone will see them sooner or later. On the following pages are samples of forms I used in my office. These forms have dual purposes. The orthodontist needs to know that the parents and child understand the magnitude of the time involved, the financial commitment, and the importance of patient cooperation. The parent needs to know what the orthodontist has planned, what it will cost in definite terms, and how they can pay it without destroying the family budget. Both are equally important if they are to remain on good terms throughout treatment. Patient satisfaction is one of the main goals of the orthodontist. Nothing builds a practice like satisfied patients and parents.

Medical /Dental History

Name_____Date of birth_____

Parent's Name_____

Address_____
Has your child:
Yes   No
____   ____ 1. Seen a physician for routine physical examination?
                  Date of last physical examination_____
                  Results_____
____   ____ 2. Ever had a health problem? If yes, explain:____
                  _____
____   ____ 3. Ever been allergic to anything? What?_____
____   ____ 4. Ever had any unfavorable reaction to medicine?
____   ____ 5. Ever had any emotional, mental, or nervous
                  disorders? If yes, explain: _____
____   ____ 6. Does your child presently take any daily
                  medication? What?_____
____   ____ 7. Please check if your child has had any of the following:
      a.___Heart disease   k____Arthritis
      b.___Rheumatic fever   l____Kidney problems
      c.___Bleeding problems m.___Speech/hearing problems
      d.___Anemia   n____Cleft lip/palate
      e.___Hepatitis   o.___Speech/hearing problems
      f____HIV   p.___Epilepsy/convulsions
      g___Diabetes   q.___AIDS
      h.___Asthma   r.___Tonsils and adenoids removed
      i____Liver problems   s.___Contact lenses
      j____Any other physical/mental problems
      Comments:_____
____   ____ 8. Has any member of your immediate family
                  had problems with any of the above?
                  What?_____

72

___   ___   9. Has your child had pain or clicking in either jaw joint?
Explain_____

___   ___   10. Does your child have difficulty chewing?
Why?_____

_____

___   ___   11. Does your child breath primarily through their mouth?

___   ___   12. Does your child have regular dental checkups?

___   ___   13. Is your child anxious to have treatment?

___   ___   14. Do other children in your family have similar problems?

___   ___   15. Does the patient ever have ringing in the ears?

___   ___   16. Is there any history of trauma to the teeth or jaws? Explain_____

_____

___   ___   17. Medical, dental or surgical problems not covered on this form?
Yes, please describe:_____

_____

___   ___   18. Has the patient had previous orthodontic consultation?

_____   _____

Responsible Party Signature   Printed Name   Date

G. Ray Callahan, DDS MS

Federal Truth in Lending Disclosure Statement for Professional Services

Date_____

Patient Name_____Parent Name_____

Address_____

Orthodontic Services

1. Cash Price (Professional fee) $_____
2. Less: Cash Down Payment (Initial fee) $_____
3. Unpaid Balance of Cash Price $_____

4. Amount Financed $_____

(Note: There will be one and one half percent interest charged per month on any overdue amount)
The amount financed shown above, is payable in equal monthly installments of $_____. The first installment being payable on _____, 20__, and all subsequent installmentsbefore the last working day of each consecutive month until paid in full.

I HEREBY CERTIFY, that I have read and received a copy of

the aforegoing Disclosure Statement this____day

of_____, 20_____.

_____

(Signature of Responsible Party)

Informed Consent for the Orthodontic Patient[9]

Orthodontics

An exciting treatment that can provide: better health and comfort, improved appearance and enhanced self-esteem. As a general rule, positive orthodontic results can be achieved by informed and cooperative patients. Thus, the following information is routinely supplied to all who are considering orthodontic treatment. While recognizing the benefits of healthy teeth and a pleasing smile, you should also be aware that orthodontic treatment has limitations and potential risks. These are seldom serious enough to indicate that treatment should be avoided, but they should be considered in making the decision whether or not to undergo orthodontic treatment. Orthodontic treatment usually proceeds as planned; however, as in all areas of the healing arts, results cannot be guaranteed, nor can all consequences be anticipated.

Orthodontics plays an important role in improving one's oral health, and in achieving balance and harmony between the teeth and face for a beautiful, healthy smile. Because of individual conditions present and the limitations of treatment imposed by nature, each specific benefit may not be attainable for every patient. The unknown factor in any orthodontic correction is the response of the patient to the orthodontic treatment.

Orthodontics strives to improve the bite by helping to direct the forces placed on teeth, thus protecting them from trauma during ordinary everyday activities, such as chewing. Orthodontics distributes the forces of chewing throughout the mouth to minimize stress on bones, roots, gum tissue and jaw joints. Orthodontic treatment may eliminate potential dental problems; including abnormal tooth wear. It may also reduce

---

[9] The American Association of Orthodontists possesses the copyright to the "Informed Consent" and it may not be reproduced without permission

75

tooth decay and future periodontal problems by making it easier to care for the teeth and gums by aiding good oral hygiene.

Risks

All forms of medical and dental treatment, including orthodontics have risks and limitations. Fortunately, complications are infrequent in orthdontics, and when they do occur, they are usually of minor consequence. Nevertheless, they should be taken into account in deciding whether to undergo orthodontic treatment. Some of the primary concerns involved in orthodontic treatment may include:

1. Tooth decay, gum disease, or permanent white markings (decalcification) on the teeth can occur, particularly if the orthodontic patient eats foods containing excessive sugar and/or does not brush his/her teeth frequently and properly. These same problems can occur without orthodontic treatment, but the risk is greater to an individual wearing braces or other appliances. These problems may be aggravated if the patient has not had the benefit of fluoridated water or its substitute.

2. In some patients, the roots of some teeth may be shortened during orthodontic treatment. Usually this shortening is minimal and does not have significant consequences, but on rare occasions it may become a threat to the longevity, stability and/or mobility of the teeth involved.

3. The bone and gum tissue which support the teeth may be affected by orthodontic tooth movement if an unhealthy condition already exists, and in some rare cases where it doesn't. In general, however, orthodontic treatment lessens the possibility of tooth loss or gum infection due to misalignment of the teeth or jaws. Inflammation of gum tissue and loss of supporting bone can occur particularly if bacterial plaque is not removed daily through good oral hygiene.

4. Teeth may have a tendency to change their positions after treatment. Proper wearing of retainers should reduce this tendency. Throughout life the bite can change adversely from various causes, such as eruption of wisdom teeth, genetic influences which control the size of the tongue, the teeth and the jaws, growth and/or maturational changes, mouth breathing, playing of musical instruments and other oral habits - all of which may be beyond the control of the orthodontist. There are times when tooth and/or jaw position may change adversely following treatment to a degree that additional treatment is recommended. The extent of further treatment would depend on, among other things, the nature of the problem and might involve a variety of potential treatment modalities including the replacement of braces.

5. Occasionally problems may occur in the jaw joints, i.e., temporomandibular joints (TMJ), causing pain, headaches or ear problems. These problems may occur with or without orthodontic treatment. Any of the above noted symptoms should be promptly reported to the orthodontist.

6. Development and eruption of teeth is a complex process. Occasionally, primary teeth become fused to the bone (ankylosis) and will not move. This is particularly true when there is no permanent successor (tooth underneath). The fused primary tooth then remains lower than the rest of the teeth which continue to erupt during normal development. This problem can also occur with permanent teeth.

7. A tooth/teeth may have been traumatized by an accident or a tooth may have large fillings that can cause damage to the nerve of the tooth. Orthodontic tooth movement may, in some cases, aggravate this condition and in some instances necessitate root canal treatment.

8. Orthodontic appliances are composed of very small parts connected together. They could be accidentally swallowed, aspirated, or could irritate or damage the oral tissues. Cheeks and lips may be scratched or irritated by loose or broken, appliances or by blows to the mouth. Post adjustment tenderness

should be expected, and the period of tenderness or sensitivity varies with individuals and with the procedure performed. (Typical post-adjustment tenderness may last 24-48 hours.) You should inform your orthodontist of any unusual symptoms or of any broken/loose appliances, as soon as they are noted.

9. Patients may inadvertently get scratched, poked or receive an injury to a tooth with potential damage to or soreness of oral structures. Abnormal wear of the teeth is also possible if a patient grinds the teeth excessively.

10. If inappropriately handled, or when impacted, a headgear may cause injury to the face or eyes, even blindness. There have been a few reports of injury to the eyes of patients from wearing headgear. Patients are warned not to wear their headgear or appliances during times of horseplay, playing sports or other competitive activity. Although our headgears are equipped with a safety system, we urge caution at all times.

11. Oral surgery, tooth removal or orthognathic surgery (surgical realignment of jaws), may be necessary in conjunction with orthodontic treatment, especially to correct crowding or severe jaw imbalances. You should discuss the risks involved with treatment and anesthesia with your general dentist or oral surgeon before making your decision to proceed with this procedure.

12. Atypical formation of teeth, or abnormal changes in the growth of the jaws may limit our ability to achieve the desired result. At times, changes after treatment require additional treatment or, in some cases, surgery. Growth disharmony and unusual tooth formations are biological processes beyond the orthodontist's control. Growth changes that occur after active orthodontic treatment may adversely alter the treatment results.

13. The total time required to complete treatment may exceed the estimate. Excessive or deficient bone growth, poor cooperation in wearing the appliances or elastics the required hours per day, poor oral hygiene, broken appliances, missed appointments and other factors can lengthen the treatment time and can adversely affect the quality of the end result.

14. When clear or tooth colored brackets have been used, there have been some reported incidents of patients experiencing bracket breakage and/or damage to teeth, including attrition and enamel flaking or fracturing on debonding. Fractured brackets may result in remnants which might be harmful to the patient.

15. Orthodontic appliances (braces) are selected to provide a specific therapeutic result. The type of appliance, construction and material content may vary. Some patients may have allergies to component materials that may result in adverse reactions and require alteration or cessation of orthodontic treatment with corresponding limits on success of therapy. Although exceedingly rare, medical management of dental material allergies may be required.

16. Due to the wide variation in size and shape of teeth, or missing teeth, achievement of an ideal result (for example, complete closure of space) may require restorative dental treatment. The most common types of dental treatment are cosmetic bonding, crown and bridge restoration and /or periodontal therapy. You are encouraged to ask questions about adjunctive dental and medical care.

17. General medical problems, such as bone, blood or endocrine disorders, can affect orthodontic treatment. You should keep your orthodontist informed of any changes in your health.

For the vast majority of patients, orthodontic treatment is an elective procedure. One possible alternative to orthodontic treatment is no treatment at all. You could choose to accept your present oral condition and decide to live without orthodontic correction or improvement. Alternatives to orthodontic treatment for any particular patient depends on the specific nature of the individual's orthodontic problem, the size, shape and health of the teeth, the physical characteristics of the supporting structure and the patient's aesthetic considerations. Alternatives could include, but not be limited to:

1. Extraction versus treatment without extractions;

2. Orthognathic surgery versus treatment without orthognathic surgery;

3. Possible prosthetic solutions; and

4. Possible compromised approaches.

You may want to discuss possible treatment alternatives or other treatment alternatives or other treatment questions with your orthodontist prior to beginning your orthodontic care.

Surgical Considerations

If the treatment plan presented by your orthodontist includes surgical movement of the jaws as well as orthodontics, the following items should be considered in making the decision to proceed with treatment.

1. Movement of teeth with orthodontic appliances prior to the orthognathic surgery is done to position them in their respective jaws, not to correct the bite in the present jaw position. The appearance and bite may actually worsen during this phase of treatment.

2. Changing the treatment plan at the patient's request from a surgical to a non-surgical treatment can cause increased treatment time and/or a compromise in the treatment results.

3. A change in treatment plan should be discussed with your family dentist and oral surgeon.

4. Orthognathic surgery can create financial concerns. A consultation with an oral and maxillofacial surgeon before treatment begins is helpful in making the decision whether or not to proceed with the proposed treatment plan.

Record

I hereby acknowledge that the major treatment considerations and potential risks of orthodontic treatment have been presented to me. I have read and understand this form and also understand that there may be other problems that occur less frequently or are less severe, and that the actual results may be different from the anticipated results.

Dr(s)._____has(have) discussed the orthodontic treatment for_____ with me. I have been asked to make a choice about that treatment. I have been presented information to aid in the decision-making process, and I have been given the opportunity to ask the above doctor(s) all questions I have about the proposed orthodontic treatment and information contained in this form.

Consent to Undergo Orthodontic Treatment

I hereby consent to the making of diagnostic records, including x-rays, before during and following orthodontic treatment, and to the above doctor(s) and, where appropriate, staff providing orthodontic treatment described by the above doctor(s) for the above individual. I fully understand all of the risks associated with the treatment.

Authorization for the Release of Patient Information

I hereby authorize the above doctor to provide other health care providers with information regarding the above individual's orthodontic care as deemed appropriate.

G. Ray Callahan, DDS MS

I understand that once released, the above doctor(s) and staff has (have) no responsibility for any further release by the individual receiving this information.

Surgical Supplement

If the orthodontic treatment plan includes correction of the malocclusion by orthodontic appliance (braces) therapy in conjunction with orthognathic (corrective jaw) surgery, I understand that oral surgery is necessary in conjunction with the above patient's orthodontic treatment. I authorize the office(s) of the above doctor(s) to communicate with the surgeon and release information from the above patient's treatment record to the designated surgeon. I acknowledge that expenses incurred from the surgery are separate from orthodontic treatment expenses, and I will be responsible to the surgeon and hospital for all such expenses.

I understand that if I do not complete the surgical component of the treatment plan that I may have a compromised treatment result and other complications. I hereby agree not to hold the above doctor(s) and staff liable for any compromised treatment resulting from my failure for any reason to follow the treatment plan.

_____   _____

Patient's Name   Date

_____   _____

Parent or Guardian's Name   Date

_____   _____

Orthodontist   Date

PATIENT'S AUTHORIZED REPRESENTATIVE

If you are consenting to the care of another: I have the legal authority to sign this on behalf of_____

_____

    Relationship to patient

_____

    Signature   Date

_____

    Witness   Date

Optional Consent to Use of Records

I hereby give my permission for the use of orthodontic records, including photographs, made in the process of examinations, treatment, and retention for purposes of professional consultations, research, education, or publication in professional journals.

I have legal authority to sign this on behalf of:

_____

_____

                  Relationship to Patient

    Signature   Date

_____

    Witness   Date

This "Informed Consent" form has been reproduced from the American Association of Orthodontists brochure entitled "Informed Consent for the Orthodontic Patient" June, 1997. Used with permission.

G. Ray Callahan, DDS MS

The Orthodontist

Chapter Seven

How to find an Orthodontist

In the first place, an orthodontist is a dentist who has had specialty training at a university for two or three years after becoming a dentist. Dentists go into this specialty because they like to treat children as well as adults. They are superior students because competition for the few spaces in graduate school is intense, and they are exceptionally talented with their hands. Braces are very tiny, and the work is precise and demanding. Some orthodontists submit to further testing to be certified by the American Board of Orthodontics. This can only be done voluntarily after at least five years of practice experience, and involve submitting fifteen case records of patients the orthodontist has treated, passing the written examination, and appearing before the board to defend the treatment of the cases. If the orthodontist passes, he or she may add the initials "ABO" after his or her other degrees.

Most orthodontists have great rapport with children and adults alike. A busy practice is built by making friends with your patients, and winning the respect of their parents. It helps to get good results, too.

If you are going to entrust your child's care to any kind of doctor, you want to pick someone who is of good moral character, honest, personable, reliable, and well qualified. There are doctors out there who fit these qualifications. Two other factors are important. The office should be spotlessly clean and the doctor and staff should wear rubber gloves when working on patients. Check out the personnel working for your doctor. Are they nice to you? Are they friendly to your child? Are you going to be comfortable if they have some part in your or your child's treatment? Is the atmosphere of the office pleasant for you both? Is the office convenient with plenty of parking?

The most reliable way to find an orthodontist is to ask your dentist for a referral. The dentist will know the orthodontists in your area who do superior work because they see those results every day in their patient's mouths. They will know personality traits as well and try to match you with a compatible practitioner. Some orthodontists like certain age groups better than others, but this should be common knowledge to your dentist.

If you don't have a dentist, that is your first problem. Orthodontists do not do general dentistry. If you like, you can see an orthodontist first, but you will be referred to a general dentist if any fillings or other procedures are necessary.

Another way to find an orthodontist is to ask your pediatrician or family physician. They will know about the general abilities of several orthodontists, but not as well as your family dentist.

Another source of referrals is your child's friends or their parents. They will usually have an opinion on whomever their child sees. They may recommend that you see someone unknown to you. You should consider the source when you get a personal referral.

You can always look in the yellow pages under "Orthodontist". If your book only lists "Dentists", you can usually find some who specialize in orthodontics. Probably some of them will have the initials, "ABO", after their names. You'll know right away that they have taken and passed further certification, and that should be a good place to start.

There are many good orthodontists who have not taken the ABO certification so don't feel that they have any less skills than the ABO group.

Ethical Considerations

The orthodontic profession is the oldest and largest specialty in the dental profession. The American Association of Orthodontists was founded in St. Louis, Mo., in 1900. The latest figures show that there are 10,049 practicing orthodontists and about 3,500 retired. The American Association of Orthodontists has its Principles of Ethics and A Code of Professional Conduct. The primary purpose and goal is to protect the public.

This document states, "The Principles of Ethics of the American Association of Orthodontists express the specialty's recognition of its responsibilities to: the public, to patients, to other health care professionals and to colleagues. These principles guide members in the performance of their professional responsibilities and express the basic tenets of ethical and professional conduct. They call for unswerving commitment to honorable behavior, even at the sacrifice of personal advantage". If you go to an orthodontist who is a member of the AAO you should feel confident that these principles will guide whatever treatment is recommended.

Procedures are in place so that if you should move to another state or community you will be transferred to another doctor who is familiar with your appliance and technique (your orthodontist has a directory) so your treatment can continue uninterrupted. The new orthodontist will make every effort to finish your case for the balance of the original fee. Sometimes that is not possible, but they will make every effort to work it out to your satisfaction.

The Orthodontic Team

The orthodontic "team" consists of a number of special people. Of course the orthodontist originates the practice and surrounds himself or herself with most of the following auxiliaries. A receptionist greets people at the front desk, answers all phone calls and is responsible for scheduling all appointments for patients. The bookkeeper works in the business office and opens all mail, records all checks, collects and records all payments left with the receptionist, arranges all payment schedules with patients or parents, and keeps the computer up to date for all patients. The bookkeeper usually makes all bank deposits. The orthodontist needs one or two assistants to help in the operatory where the patients are treated. One assistant may be necessary for every chair. Assistants are usually graduates of a community college dental assisting program. Many orthodontists now have all treatment records on computer so there is a computer in every operatory. One of the assistants usually enters the treatment on the chart in the computer as the doctor dictates.

Orthodontists like to hire dental hygienists as assistants because they are familiar with working in the mouth, dealing with patients and are highly skilled with their hands. Orthodontists also don't usually have hygienists practicing oral hygiene in their offices so as to not furnish a service that their referring dentists furnish in their offices. It doesn't pay to take away a source of income from the dentist that you expect to send patients to you. The assistants are also responsible for taking x-rays, photographs, and impressions as well as any other orthodontic records. A laboratory person makes study models from the impressions and fabricates retainers or any necessary laboratory tasks.

Therefore, if the orthodontist has four chairs in the office there are usually at least five auxiliaries. There may be other personnel such as one or more of the following, (1) a patient education person, responsible for teaching toothbrushing, wearing of elastics and headgear, explaining functional appliances and retainers, (2) a treatment coordinator who explains the treatment plan at the consultation appointment, greets all new patients and shows them around the office, and keeps track of new patients coming into the practice to be sure they get started and not lost and (3) a records person who takes all orthodontic records rather than having the assistants do it, who traces radiographs and is responsible for ordering supplies such as film and developer for his or her department. Photographs are difficult to do consistently well so it helps to have the same person doing it all the time.

Another auxiliary found in many offices is the orthodontist's wife, especially if the orthodontist is young and hasn't started a family yet. Wives are very friendly to patients and frequently help the office to run smoothly. There are some exceptions, but on the average the other auxiliaries do not resent the doctor's wife in the office. The wife can be very good at smoothing over awkward moments when someone is upset, patient or otherwise.

G. Ray Callahan, DDS MS

Conclusion

Orthodontic treatment for a child or an adult with crooked teeth or deformed jaws can seem like a miracle. Chewing function can be restored where the patient is essentially a dental cripple. The appearance can be improved to the point to bring them into the mainstream rather than isolated on the fringe. All of these wonderful improvements can occur in anyone's life by combining the efforts of their orthodontist and other professionals.

Treatment results are almost routinely good from many aspects. We strive to improve function, have a near ideal appearance, and align the teeth correctly to restore the natural benefits of an ideal occlusion. Every case is not perfect, however, but the vast majority of cases, where the patient does his or her part, turn out very well. I hope this book can get that point (patient cooperation) across to both parents and patients.

If braces are in your future, you're in for a treat. Good Luck!!

G. Ray Callahan, DDS MS

Glossary of Orthodontic Words and Terms

ABO   American Board of Orthodontics

Abscess   The infection from a dead or dying tooth that may come through the gum tissue

Adolescence   Transitional period between the teen years and the age of majority (21)

Anesthetic   Material which may be used to numb an area of the mouth

Bite Wafer   A soft plastic material to bite on after orthodontic adjustment. It is thought to relieve tooth pain.

Canine Tooth   The third tooth from the front of the mouth

Cephalometric
Radiograph   X-ray of the head in a profile view

Cephalometric
Tracing   Pencil tracing of cephalometric radiograph on transparent acetate paper to help with the diagnosis and treatment plan

Ceramic   Very hard, translucent material used to make orthodontic brackets

Consultation	The appointment when the orthodontist meets with the patient to discuss the diagnosis
Crib	Wires bonded to teeth to prevent thumb or tongue habits.
Diagnosis	The decision the orthodontist makes about what is wrong with the patient's teeth
Diastema	The space between teeth
Equilibration	Selective spot grinding of tooth surfaces
Habits	Thumbsucking, lip biting or tongue thrusting are the most important to orthodontists
Hand Film	X-ray which can be used to assess skeletal age in a child.
Headgear	An appliance outside the mouth to put backward or forward pressure on the upper teeth
Hygienist	Professional person educated to clean teeth and handle patient education
Intra-oral	Inside the mouth
Jaw Discrepancy	Upper and Lower jaws don't fit together correctly.

Lingual	Tongue side of the teeth
Malocclusion	Literally, bad bite or poor arrangement of teeth.
Mandibular Prognathism	Lower jaw grows too far forward
Midpalatal Suture	Where the bone joins together in the roof of the mouth.
Myofunctional Therapists	Specially trained people who treat muscle problems in the mouth, face and neck
Occlusion	How the teeth bite together
Open Bite	Upper and lower teeth don't meet in a certain area.
Orthognathic	Straight jaws
Overbite	The amount the upper front teeth overlap the lower front teeth in a vertical direction
Overjet	The amount the upper front teeth stick out horizontally forward of the lower front teeth

Periodontal Problems	Damage to ligaments, bone or tissue around the teeth.
Radiograph	X-ray
Retention	Holding teeth in position when they're loose after treatment until they tighten up again
Rubber Bands	Tiny elastic bands to connect two areas of the braces to produce specific movements
Rubber Gloves	Very thin latex gloves worn by doctors and nurses
Study Models	Plaster reproductions of the teeth and gums
Supernumerary teeth	Extra tooth or teeth above the normal number
Tongue Thrust	Action of the tongue pushing forward during the swallow

Acknowledgments

Thanks to David Sinow, BA, MA, JD, PhD, friend, financial advisor, father of two of my patients and the originator of the idea for this book. David was a close neighbor of ours in Mahomet, Illinois. He is a dedicated school board member, a University Professor of Finance, and president of a bank that he founded. I owe David a great debt of gratitude.

I'm grateful to Diana McDonald, BA, MA, who edited this book. Diana has been putting my words into logical sequence from the very beginning of this book (1997). She is a very good English Instructor at Parkland College, but (lucky for me) she loves to edit books. She also lives in Mahomet, Illinois with her family.

I also wish to thank and acknowledge the talents of Julie LaFleur R.T.R., the artist who drew the illustrations. She is employed as an X-ray technician in my son's orthopedic surgery office. When I was searching for an illustrator, he praised her highly for drawings she had done for him. His opinion is well founded.

I owe my wife, Kae Callahan, for 42 years of wedded bliss. I can't thank her enough for the many times she has read this manuscript and given me constructive criticism. Whenever I lapsed into "dental-speak" she called me on it and then I would have to rewrite it in plain English. Her love and encouragement kept me on track.

I'm very grateful to our children for giving us such wonderful grandchildren. Our daughter Kenda has three children: AnnaKae (6), Nikolas (5), and William (2). Our older son Bert also has three children: Jason (10), Ryan (8) and Sarah (5). Our younger son Bill has only one child, a daughter named Devin Esther who was born on August 15, 2000. Bill deserves a special thank you for sharing his ingenious computer skills and helping me organize this book.

A special tribute goes to my parents, Bert and Elsie Callahan for their emphasis on education from my earliest memories. When I was in high school, there was no question if I was going to college, only where. My parents both graduated from high school (not bad in 1923), but my Dad was the only one of ten children in his family to do so. He wanted to be a physician and now his namesake has accomplished that goal.

A special thanks to Kae's parents, Dr. Will and Lois Clark for their love and friendship over these many years. At ages 96 and 93, respectively, they have been an inspiration to all of us. They are mentally and physically terrific. Will's parents homesteaded in South Dakota in 1903. He retired as a Colonel in the Army Dental Corps in 1964. Lois is a Northwestern University graduate in Dental Hygiene from Iowa. They have been married 67 years.

I want to thank Dr. Thomas Triller of Beaver Dam, Wisconsin and Dr. Gene King of Champaign, Illinois for reading this manuscript and offering constructive criticism.

And last but not least I want to thank my grandchildren for posing for my illustrations. Even though the girls do not suck their thumbs and the boys are too young for headgear, they posed readily. The youngest does use the pacifier.

ABOUT THE AUTHOR

Dr. Ray Callahan is a small town boy from two miles north of Ridgefarm, Illinois. He graduated from high school in 1950. The University of Illinois was his college choice, which he attended on an academic scholarship he won on a competitive examination. Dentistry became his chosen field so he attended the University of Illinois College of Dentistry in Chicago for four years and graduated in 1957. The U.S. Military was on everyone's agenda in those days so he served as a dentist in the Army for three years including a year in Korea. Ray's first child was born while he was in Korea so he didn't see her for the first five months. After military service Dr. Callahan was one of the ten out of six-hundred applicants who were accepted into orthodontic training at Northwestern University, also in Chicago.

In February, 1962, he opened a solo practice in Champaign, Illinois. In 1970 he became part of a group practice of three orthodontists. After over twenty years the group gradually broke up and Dr. Callahan sold his practice in 1996 and retired. In early 1997, writing became his primary pastime. His friend and financial advisor, Dr. David Sinow, came up with the suggestion to write this book, because he hadn't known what to expect when he brought his children to Dr. Callahan for orthodontic treatment. This book is the result of three years of research, writing and rewriting.

Dr. Callahan has been married to his wife, Kae, for forty-two years. They have three children: Kenda, Bert and Bill. Kenda is a pharmacist, married to a general dentist (Art), Bert is an orthopedic surgeon, married to a physical therapist (Debbie), and Bill is an artist, a graduate of the Chicago Art Institute, and married to a communications graduate of Iowa (Kim).

www.ingramcontent.com/pod-product-compliance
Lightning Source LLC
Chambersburg PA
CBHW050403290526
45786CB00003B/1114